"Resilience feels like an exotic rari[...]
joyful and faithful, yet so often we don't know how. Lewis and Sarah Allen shine the light of the gospel onto our everyday lives, showing how we can grow spiritual muscle amid the practical challenges we face. Here is wisdom and comfort for all who want to endure and thrive in Christ."

    **Michael Reeves,** President and Professor of Theology, Union School of Theology; author, *Rejoice and Tremble and Gospel People*

"Gentle yet firm where it needs to be, practical and biblical, this book is filled with actionable insights for the struggling Christian to (re)discover resilient faith!"

    **Josh Moody,** Senior Pastor, College Church, Wheaton, Illinois; President, God Centered Life Ministries

"Such wisdom! Lewis and Sarah Allen will arm you with gospel weaponry to apply to the whole of life, including habits in food, exercise, sleep, relationships, and spiritual discipline—spurring you on to retreat to Christ and thus grow in stamina. This book gave me the gospel backbone to face past hurts, especially those wrapped around the church, and move on to greater resilience, love, and service."

    **Natalie Brand,** Bible teacher; author, *Prone to Wander: Grace for the Lukewarm and Apathetic*

"Realistic, honest, and saturated in Scripture, Lewis and Sarah Allen gently challenge us to have the courage to defy our culture, deny ourselves, and follow Christ when we would rather stay on the sofa."

    **Jonty and Linda Allcock,** Pastor, The Globe Church, Central London, United Kingdom; author, *Impossible Commands*; and his wife, Linda, author, *Deeper Still* and *Head Heart Hands*

*Resilient Faith*

# Resilient Faith

*Learning to Rely on Jesus in the Struggles of Life*

## Lewis and Sarah Allen

WHEATON, ILLINOIS

---

**Library of Congress Cataloging-in-Publication Data**

Names: Allen, Lewis, 1971– author. | Allen, Sarah, 1971– author.
Title: Resilient faith: learning to rely on Jesus in the struggles of life / Lewis Allen and Sarah Allen.
Description: Wheaton, Illinois: Crossway, 2022. | Includes bibliographical references and index.
Identifiers: LCCN 2021052184 (print) | LCCN 2021052185 (ebook) | ISBN 9781433577987
    (trade paperback) | ISBN 9781433577994 (pdf) | ISBN 9781433578007 (mobipocket) | ISBN
    9781433578014 (epub)
Subjects: LCSH: Resilience (Personality trait)—Religious aspects—Christianity. | Trust in
    God—Christianity.
Classification: LCC BV4597.58.R47 A45 2022 (print) | LCC BV4597.58.R47 (ebook) | DDC
    233/.5–dc23/eng/20211130
LC record available at https://lccn.loc.gov/2021052184
LC ebook record available at https://lccn.loc.gov/2021052185

---

Crossway is a publishing ministry of Good News Publishers.

BP          32   31   30   29   28   27   26   25   24   23
15   14   13   12   11   10   9   8   7   6   5   4   3   2   1

*To all of the young adults we've shared our lives with and received so much from over the last 25 years, and to our five precious children. We are so much richer through God's grace in your lives. "May the Lord direct your hearts to the love of God and to the steadfastness of Christ" (2 Thess. 3:5).*

*Let us run with perseverance the race marked out for us,*
*fixing our eyes on Jesus, the pioneer and perfecter of faith.*
*For the joy set before him he endured the cross, scorning its*
*shame, and sat down at the right hand of the throne of God.*

HEBREWS 12:1–2 NIV

# Contents

Introduction: The Enduring Gospel    *1*

PART 1: RETREAT

1  Where Troubles Take Us: Learning to Retreat Like Jesus    *9*

2  The All-Seeing, All-Caring Lord: Secure in the Savior    *16*

3  Step Out: Forward with Jesus Is Always the Right
Direction    *24*

PART 2: YOU CAN STOP NOW!

4  One Day: The Sunday Gift    *35*

5  Every Day: The Rest That Restores    *43*

PART 3: HOPE-FULL

6  Those Who Hope in the Lord: Fix Your Hope on
Easter Truth    *57*

7  The Hope of Heaven: Glory Is Waiting for Us    *64*

8  Hope Today: Living with the Hope of Glory    *70*

PART 4: BODY LIFE

9   Appetite: Bringing Our Habits and Desires to Jesus   *79*

10  Body Work: How Everything We Do Matters to God   *90*

PART 5: THE RESILIENT GOSPEL

11  The Courage of Grace: Think, Feel, Fight   *101*

12  Facing the Enemy: Our Tempter and Our Shield   *108*

13  Battle Lines: Confident in Jesus's Righteousness   *115*

PART 6: GOD'S WORD: PRIZING THE POWER

14  The Sharp Edge: Do You Know the Power of
    God's Word?   *125*

15  Confession Time: Bring Your Heart to the God
    Who Cares   *131*

16  Truth Wins: Prizing the Bible   *137*

PART 7: GOD'S WORD: HEARTS AND HABITS

17  Hold On! Creating and Keeping Healthy Bible
    Habits   *147*

18  Take It to Heart: God's Word for Our Deep Needs   *153*

19  Sharing the Word: Learning to Minister Jesus in
    How We Speak   *160*

PART 8: PRAYING

20  Depend: Discover the Freedom of Relying on
    the Lord   *169*

21  The Weak and the Strong: How Grace Changes a
    Praying Heart  *176*

22  The Spirit Is Here: Experiencing the Spirit as We Pray  *183*


PART 9: THE CHURCH

23  Sharing Worship: The Church Meets Her Lord  *193*

24  Leaning In: Enjoying Family Life Together  *200*

25  Resilient through Serving: The Spirit Sustains and
    Grows Jesus's Servants  *208*


    Conclusion: And So?  *215*
    Notes  *217*
    General Index  *221*
    Scripture Index  *225*

Introduction

# The Enduring Gospel

Spirit-Filled and Stumbling?

WE'VE GOT A BOX in our home where we keep a battered blue and white badge. Anyone of a certain age who grew up in the UK will probably recognize it. It marks me (Sarah) out as having been a runner-up in a competition organized by the children's TV show *Blue Peter*. To have a Blue Peter badge in the early 1980s meant that you were a winner!

Don't you just love success? Maybe somewhere you have a certificate or a trophy that brings back a rush of happy memories. You've worked hard at something, and you've succeeded at it. People have noticed your talents, and you've made progress at what you've set your heart on. Success is sweet, and life sometimes is very sweet. You've got the badge to prove it.

So often, though, life can be hard and bitter. We're writing this book near the end of 2021. The COVID-19 pandemic has caused immense and international devastation over the past two years. Some have been personally affected by illness and bereavement. All have had personal freedom severely restricted. We've been reminded that, despite rapidly improving technology, life is fragile, the unexpected can happen, and people are unreliable. And it's not just other people who are unreliable, but perhaps you've discovered you're unreliable too. One day you think you'll achieve great things, but then the next day, it's all you can do to crawl out of bed. Hard situations show how weak we all are.

This weakness can be confusing if you're a Christian. You know that you are a child of God, filled with his Spirit. Your Bible teaches you that God is for you, but when trials come, you stumble and feel as though you are falling. Is your faith all that you thought it was?

### Real World

We have been happily married for over twenty-five years and have been involved in ministry together for even longer. We're not immune, however, to the struggles of feeling weary and weak. Dealing with our own problems, serving other people, and just being part of a family means that very often we both feel out of our depth, confused and failing. Sometimes other people see our cracks; sometimes they don't.

Our five children are now in or approaching young adulthood. As we watch and support them, we've realized that life for them and the young adults in our church is so much harder than it was for us at the same stage. The world is a far less stable place, and young adults are bearing the brunt of the instability. A fragile world makes for fragile minds and hearts. For example, in both the US and the UK the proportion of students who reported a mental health difficulty in 2021 was around 50 percent, an enormous increase from the 20 percent who identified in this way in 2014.[1] The privileges previously taken for granted—housing, careers, savings, health care—are in scant supply for today's young adults.

Fortunately, it seems easier than ever before to raise your hand and say, "I'm struggling," and that's no bad thing. There are countless celebrities and sports people who have been applauded for honesty and courage in acknowledging their weaknesses. But what happens next? How do they (and you) keep going when pain comes? Or how do you get back on your feet when you feel as though you've been floored? And how does our Christian faith make a real difference? Before you is a journey into distinctively Christian resilient faith and living. It's a way marked out by our persevering Savior, Jesus Christ, and he has all the resources needed to help all of us make it to the end with a confident faith in him.

## Real Resilience

This book is written out of our own personal challenges, joys, and disappointments in work, relationships, and church. It also comes out of our work supporting young adults who are struggling to stand firm, Christian as well as non-Christian. We've seen that in times of trial, what's needed more than anything else is *resilience*, the ability to weather the storm and keep going.

For the Christian, resilience is about more than grittiness or self-care. It is about standing firm in your faith and keeping on following Jesus. Thirty-one times the New Testament uses the Greek word *hypomene*. The sense of it is covered by our words "patient-endurance," "perseverance," and "steadfastness." This is the grace-shaped habit of keeping on trusting Christ even when life is hard, of relying on God's power to obey Jesus in difficult times.

So here in this book, we'll be focusing on developing resilient faith. There are nine main sections, each with two or three mini chapters. Some chapters are written by Sarah, some by Lewis. We suggest that you take one chapter a day or perhaps ponder a part each week. You could give yourself the added challenge of reading this book with a friend. Together, aim to grow as you discuss and pray through what you read and learn in this book. Discipleship is always best shared!

Some of what we talk about will help you explore the assumptions you have about life—for example, the place of rest, work, leisure, and habits in the life of faith. We explore the attitudes and behaviors that will help you grow in engaging with God's word, praying, being part of the church, and serving the Lord. We are sure that resilient faith, which the Holy Spirit is forming in all of us, is shaped as we bring all of life under the loving and gentle authority of our gracious Lord.

In the pages ahead we illustrate some of the challenges Christians face by introducing you to some characters, their struggles and faith. These aren't specific individuals; instead, we've put together traits and situations from a range of people we've known over years of ministry.

The Bible passage that more than any other shapes what's ahead is Ephesians 6:10–18. Our central chapters explore this passage of Scripture in some detail. Paul sets before the Ephesian believers the idea that the Christian life is a battle Christians are commanded to fight. If Christians are to develop and stand with a resilient faith, we all must take up the spiritual weapons and armor that Paul details. If we step out of the battle, pretend that the devil isn't real, or assume that the Christian life is easy, we've lost. If we fight the battle, experiencing in Winston Churchill's famous phrase, "toil, tears, and sweat," we'll discover that we're actually standing firm through the working of God's power. We are being resilient in his strength.

We want to help you put on the armor that God provides so that you can stand firm in both the gut-wrenching shocks of life and in the energy-draining day-to-day. More than anything, we want to encourage you that God is really for you in this journey. As you learn to stand in your faith, you will see how much you are loved and safe in Christ, can be confident in the Father's plan for you, and are empowered by his indwelling Spirit. There is truly no joy as deep as standing firm in faith in the Lord (2 Cor. 1:24).

Let's go!

PART 1

———————

# RETREAT

Trouble comes to everyone. You just have to wait. It might take a while and appear as a sudden blow, or it may have been keeping you company for longer than you can remember. When any of us meet trouble, we discover that life isn't a cartoon in which crisis comes neatly packaged and labeled, an obstacle to jump over on the way to a happy ending. Trouble—whether unemployment, ill health, loneliness, anxiety, or any of the everyday difficulties we all face—changes the way we behave toward God and toward other people.

Our dog Laurie is a big, hairy lurcher. He can run like the wind and loves to play with our kids, though strangers might back away when he comes bounding up, muddy and eager to say *Hi!*, all fangs and big paws. But in November, when fireworks are let off to celebrate Diwali and Guy Fawkes Night, Laurie hides because he's a wreck. No matter how soft and calming our voices are or how many times he's heard the bangs and whistles, he squeezes himself into the tightest spot he can find behind the sofa or under my desk and shivers. He retreats.

You and I are the same. When trouble arrives, we very often retreat, brushing off the comfort that is available and shrinking ourselves in an attempt to stay safe. For an hour or two during fireworks that might not be a bad strategy for a dog. But hiding away for weeks and months under the duvet or online does real damage to us.

In these next three chapters, we'll start by looking at how Christians sometimes retreat in stressful situations. Then you'll learn from Jesus other ways of responding besides retreat. He entered a world of trouble and can show you how to stand and face difficulty. What's more, he offers you the strength to do it.

# 1

# Where Troubles Take Us

### Learning to Retreat Like Jesus

*. . . Jesus, the founder and perfecter of our faith.*

HEBREWS 12:2

SOMETIMES WHEN someone asks me how I'm doing, I (Sarah) answer, "I'm fine," when I'm not. That might be because it's the wrong time or place or even the wrong person to talk to. But sometimes it is because I just don't want to face the issues all around me. I don't want to expose myself to other people's help. I kid myself that I've got my own strategies for dealing with my problems. I think that I'm all right on my own.

## Pressure Points

There was a time when my friend Nell thought exactly the same. While drowning in the demands of college deadlines, she told me she was fine and put on a fake smile. She stopped replying to my texts and didn't pick up the phone. She didn't only push me away, she pushed the God she loved away too. She couldn't concentrate when she tried to pray, so she stopped praying. Reading her Bible was overwhelming, so she stopped that too. Still, she turned up at church and Bible study. She knew all the right answers to give in discussion and polite conversation. Ask her how she was doing, and the reply would come back, "I'm all right . . . really. How are you?" But inside, she grew more and more distressed.

Nell's strategy of masking her difficulties by smiling wasn't working for her. She had felt that time was what she needed and that being on her own would help. She thought that if she could get through this crisis on her own, it would be easier and less messy. But her experience of retreating from church friends and the Lord proved scary. In the end, she came to realize that separation is death-like. Retreating into yourself and relying on yourself, she discovered, can feel deathly.

### How Jesus Responded to Pressure

It was good news for Nell to discover that Jesus retreated at times, but that his retreats weren't about panic or self-reliance. In Matthew 13–14, we hear about some of the pressures Jesus was under. First, he was in Nazareth, his hometown, but although people were amazed at his teaching, they rejected it and took offense (Matt. 13:53–58). Second, he heard that his cousin, John the Baptist, had been beheaded by Herod, and that Herod was now terrified that Jesus was actually John brought back to life (Matt. 14:1–12). Rejection, grief, and perhaps concern about Herod's next move must have created the temptation for Jesus to despair. We know that Jesus was tempted in the wilderness (see Matt. 4:1–11). But think about this: he faced the human realities of stress and trouble and sorrow throughout his life. Temptation for him must have been ever present. He was *fully* human in *every* way. And so, he reacted to these pressures in a fully human, fully sinless way by retreating into relationship.

In Matthew 14:13, Jesus "withdrew . . . to a desolate place by himself" and, as he was interrupted, later he went farther, escaping "up on the mountain by himself to pray . . . he was there alone" (14:23). Matthew couldn't be clearer about Jesus's retreat to be away from people to be with his God, on whom, in his human nature, he depended. Exposed on the mountain in all his human vulnerability, Jesus could pour out his heart and be understood. He could be comforted through knowing his Father.

Of course, intimate dependence and comfort is what you want when you're stressed, isn't it? That *is* what we all yearn for. And it is obvious that seeking God's help is what we should do, isn't it? Apart from all the other useful strategies we will take time to explore in the course of this book, taking time to rest consciously in God's love has to be number one. There are no substitutes.

Does this truth sting a bit? Perhaps (as I do) you feel regret or sadness or even guilt as you see Jesus's perfect response to pressure, and as you reflect on your own kind of retreat. Rather than retreating into relationship with our heavenly Father, we so often hide in distraction and worse. Whether your go-to distraction is binge-watching, binge-eating, compulsive shopping, or something darker, or the (often, but not always) healthier options of fiction, gaming, crafting, social-media, or exercise—it still isn't prayer, or at least, not in-depth prayer. The issue, very often, for us Christians isn't that we don't know what to do, but that we don't do what we know is best.

## Turning Back—to Him

What then are we to do?

Reflect for a moment on why Jesus would have journeyed to the mountaintop in the dark. God is love: the Son and Father and the Holy Spirit are always one in essence and united in joyful, delighting, superabounding love. Now incarnated in a limited body, Jesus went to spend time with his heavenly Father, to find rest in this love. He did it because it was the best thing for a tempted and pressured man to do.

This loving retreat, what one theologian has called "a perfect openness,"[2] was an expression of obedience. As a perfect man, Jesus obeyed his Father by remaining in his love (John 15:10). To love God, for him (and for us as his followers) means seeking to obey; to obey means persevering in love. So often, the right-thing-to-do seems to us like drudgery. Dull but necessary, like cleaning the bathroom or drinking plenty of water, writing thank-you notes or checking the oil in the car. But Jesus shows us here that to obey is to love. He obeyed because he loves his Father, and he loves us. Now that is a remarkable thought! Here I am at my desk, typing on a laptop in a Yorkshire town on a snowy February evening. Jesus walked up a mountain in the warmth of a Galilean spring two thousand years ago, and he did it out of love for me. This loving obedience of his, as he retreated to wrestle in prayer, was part of the righteous life he lived that I and so many millions more might know him now and into eternity.

In Romans 5:19, Paul tells us that "through the obedience of the one man the many will be made righteous" (NIV). This means that the minute-by-minute obedience of Jesus's earthly life, and the ultimate obedience of dying on the cross, have changed the identity of all who have been joined to him by faith. If you've put your trust in him, you're joined to him, and if you're joined to him, you're given his righteousness. It's as if you now have an ID card stamped "righteous." All the boxes you've ticked and those you've left blank are now superimposed by that stamp. Righteous.

So how does this help you when you yet again turn your eyes away from the Bible on the shelf or ignore the texts and calls of your Christian brothers and sisters? Well, for a start, it tells you that's not who you are. Christians have been called righteous. And to be righteous is to be connected and dependent, not disconnected and self-reliant.

This means that turning to Jesus in trial or in worry or even in boredom is to walk through a door he has already opened for you by his own obedience. You might feel the battle to concentrate or struggle to be honest about the state you've slipped into but turning to Jesus means entering his loving embrace. Jesus did the right things you couldn't and wouldn't do, and this means that now you can take that step into conscious dependence on him. How do you start? Perhaps by confessing the independence that has kept you from coming to him and the desire you have to keep away from God and his holiness. You must ask him to give you a hunger to keep turning back to him and for the day-by-day strength to form new habits of reliance.

Nell's recognition that separation was doing her no good was the start of rediscovering her strength in the Lord. It wasn't an easy start, and there have been quite a few backward steps and pauses in her journey so far. Through God's help, she's learning to keep retreating to God, to speak honestly with her Lord about where she is. That step has led to her speaking honestly to a few other people too. Knowing their support, she has found that her practical problems aren't so overwhelming as they once seemed.

## Reflect

1. In what ways do you hide from difficulties? What are some habits that you have developed as a way of avoiding dependence on others or on the Lord?

2. Reflect prayerfully on these extraordinary verses from Hebrews:

Therefore, since we have a great high priest who has ascended into heaven, Jesus the Son of God, let us hold firmly to the faith we profess. For we do not have a high priest who is unable to empathize with our weaknesses, but we have one who has been tempted in every way, just as we are—yet he did not sin. Let us then approach God's throne of grace with confidence, so that we may receive mercy and find grace to help us in our time of need. (Heb. 4:14–16 NIV)

During the days of Jesus' life on earth, he offered up prayers and petitions with fervent cries and tears to the one who could save him from death, and he was heard because of his reverent submission. (Heb. 5:7 NIV)

Notice how Jesus is shown in these verses. He knows what it is like to be tempted and to be dependent. He knows how hard prayer is. And through all of this, he conquered to become the priest you need. His power is made perfect in weakness.

3. What is one new habit you'd like to develop to cultivate dependence on God and fellow Christians? Write it down and consider what you need to change. Is there a Christian friend you need to share your struggles with? Could you ask someone from church to check up on how you are really doing?

### Pray

*Lord Jesus, I thank you that you showed us by your life what it means to rely on your perfect Father. I thank you that you pray for me in all my weakness.*

*Heavenly Father, I thank you that you hear your Son's eternal prayer and save those who come to him.*

*Holy Spirit, I thank you that you have been sent to strengthen all who ask for help in Jesus's name.*

*Help me rely on you, Lord God, and give me the desire and will to keep turning to you. Help me to be honest with others about my struggles and ready to receive help.*

*All this I pray, in Jesus's name and through the power of the Holy Spirit, amen.*

# 2

# The All-Seeing, All-Caring Lord

## Secure in the Savior

*I have seen him who looks after me.*

GENESIS 16:13

EVERY SO OFTEN I (Sarah) see a story in the news about sinkholes. Tiny cracks slowly appear in a pavement or a road, then suddenly a hole opens up and a car, house, or perhaps a person plummets down. The sinkholes are normally not that deep, but the devastation can be horrible. Last summer, I saw footage of a man waiting for a bus in New York City when a sinkhole suddenly opened up beneath him. One moment the man was standing silently on a bustling sidewalk; the next moment he was in fifteen feet of darkness, cold and wet and surrounded by rats!

## Going Under?

It's easy to see how our troubles can feel like a sinkhole. We might fall into them when we're just going about our business. Though we may be physically near everyone else, we are stuck in a different and scary world. In this part, we've already thought about our inclination to pull back and withdraw into self-reliance when we hit difficulty. Here I want us to think about the temptation toward destructive self-pity: the instinct we all feel to obsess about ourselves, our needs, and our pain while forgetting the needs of others.

In pain it is easy to keep running over our sorrows, playing to ourselves (and perhaps to others) a soundtrack of grievances and hurts. The "If only . . . ," "Why me?," "Not again," "This is all so awful!" and "She always . . . " thoughts run on loop, sometimes with an added "It's not my fault," or "It's so unfair." This narrative makes the walls of our sinkhole seem steeper and slimier. It becomes harder and harder to climb out, and the darkness presses in.

I've found that a difficulty can come to define who I am; it dominates my social media feed, what I read, and the songs I listen to. Life becomes all about my particular kind of hardship. I've looked out on others and thought, "You won't understand. You don't know what it is like!" Have you ever found yourself in a similar situation?

In these situations it then becomes tempting to play Top Trumps of suffering. Do you remember that card game? When our children were younger, we had a dinosaur Top Trumps pack. There was a card for each species with a terrifying picture and also scores for different characteristics—say, fighting power, adaptability, or size. In a similar way we rank and compare our troubles to decide who most deserves our compassion, and how much of it to give. Very often, our troubles rank highest of all. *I'm the one who needs pity!* What's more, *I need all the pity I've got* so there's not much left over for anyone else—at least not much for people outside our immediate circles or who might demand much from us or who don't share our suffering score.

Please don't misunderstand me here. We've just seen in our last chapter how Jesus wrestled in prayer, so there's certainly a place in the Christian life for lament and honesty about pain and hardship. We absolutely must recognize our griefs, share them with others, and retreat into the love of God. There's a difference, though, between an honest expression of pain brought to the Lord and self-centered pity.

## The All-Seeing Savior We All Need

Let's look at what happens when Jesus retreats. The first time in Matthew 14, he arrives at the solitary place he's heading for but is met by crowds who have tracked him down wanting miracles and healing. What does he do? Though he is grieving and under pressure, his heart responds. "He had compassion on them and healed their sick" (v. 14). In Mark's version of the event, the reason for this compassion is added. Jesus sees that the crowds "were like sheep without a shepherd" (Mark 6:34). He's not moved by their need for physical help so much as by their lostness. These crowds are wandering without the direction and protection a shepherd could bring. They are in danger. So he heals, teaches, and later feeds them fish and bread. Jesus's retreat has been interrupted by the needs of demanding crowds. They do not deserve his attention.

They've done nothing to earn it. They evidently had little interest in this miracle-worker except what they could get from him for their daily needs. But Jesus gives them love and help, because he understands their deep needs. Despite his own burdens, he is able to reach out.

The second time Jesus withdraws (straight after feeding the crowds), he does get to pray, but then something similar happens (Matt. 14:22–33). After praying all through the night, he sees his disciples struggling. They are in their boat "a long way from the land, beaten by the waves, for the wind was against them" (v. 24). Do these men, whom he's already given so much attention, need it again now? Jesus didn't have to go out to them, but he does, leaving the quiet of the mountain for a stormy lake and struggling friends. This time it is Jesus who does the interrupting as he disturbs the disciples in their trouble and brings them real peace.

Can you see the pattern? Jesus retreats and then goes out to offer his strength to people, whether they are looking for him or not. This may be a great pattern for us Christians to follow, but it's far better than simply a good example. It's good news for you, whether you feel that you're in a sinkhole or not, because it means you have Jesus's help and strength. We all need Jesus to shepherd us, leading, feeding, and protecting. His pity and compassion toward his sheep can interrupt our self-pity and self-absorption. Knowing that the ruler of the universe loves us all, that he is a Father who "shows compassion to his children," "knows our frame," and "remembers that we are dust," as David tells us in Psalm 103:13–14, brings us all great liberation. If the Lord is truly compassionate toward us, we have no need to pity ourselves. We can trust him.

When things are difficult for my good friend Steve, he struggles to get out of bed. The alarm may go off, but the duvet is warm, and it's somehow more comfortable to stay in bed, obsessing about hard situations than to get up, make coffee, and start the day with God's word. For Steve, self-absorption acts as a comfort blanket, wrapping him up and making him feel safe. Dwelling on hardships is just a way of hiding from them. It also keeps Steve at the center. Focusing on what is wrong without dealing with it can be strangely comforting, though it achieves nothing.

Steve knows, however, that the Lord is compassionate, and this knowledge helps break his habit of self-absorption. How does this work? It starts with the knowledge that God sees him (and us).

This truth that God sees us runs as a golden thread throughout Scripture. God sees the wickedness of Noah's day and acts to save (Genesis 6–8); he sees wretched, abandoned Hagar, who is the first to name God, calling him "a God of seeing" (Gen. 16:13); he sees the suffering of the enslaved Israelites in Egypt and is concerned (Ex. 3:7). Throughout the Psalms and the Prophets is the certainty that the Lord sees humanity in its sin and suffering (for example, Pss. 33:12–15; 38:9; 139:3; Jer. 1:12). Then, as Jesus arrives in the Gospels, his kingdom teaching turns again and again to "your Father who sees in secret" and who even notices the tiny sparrow's fall (Matt. 6:4, 6, 18; 10:29). Our God looks and sees and cares. As Hagar said, "I have seen him who looks after me," her desperation turning to awe and trust (Gen. 16:13), we have also seen the same God and seen the depths of his sacrificial love for us in Christ.

Just as in Matthew 14, Jesus sees the crowds and his disciples and understands their needs, so he sees you and understands your needs. Jesus sees you when you don't want to get out of bed. He sees you in your self-pity, and his pity and love are greater than your own for yourself. He sees the trouble you're in—including your failure to respond rightly to your trouble—and he has compassion.

When Jesus goes out to his disciples on the lake, his arrival disturbs them, but he actually comes to bring strength. He says to them, "Take heart; it is I. Do not be afraid" (Matt. 14:27). Jesus deals with Peter's strange mix of enthusiasm, challenge, and doubt expressed in his shout, "*If* it is you, command me to come to you on the water" (v. 28), by doing what Peter asks. Jesus commands Peter to come. And on that miraculous walk, Peter is taught an important lesson. Peter has to look at Jesus, the one who sees him, and not at the dark water. Safety lies in looking to Jesus.

When you know this (and you'll need to learn this lesson again and again), you can start looking to the needs of others. Getting out from under the comfort-blanket of self-pity by remembering that Jesus really does care about your situation means that you'll have headspace to have compassion for your family or friends. If you are no longer playing the Top Trumps suffering game or keeping note of who has shown you the compassion you think you deserve, then you're much more free. Troubles will carry on, for sure, but you can make that phone call or pray or sign up to serve. You can share the compassion that you've received, knowing that you don't have to be sorted out first.

## Reflect

1. What are your sinkhole moments? Are there particular times in the day when you can become self-absorbed? Are there practical

things you could do to interrupt your thinking patterns at these times—perhaps putting on some Christian music or getting outside for a walk?

2. Reflect on and, if you can, memorize this verse:

Put on then, as God's chosen ones, holy and beloved, compassionate hearts, kindness, humility, meekness, and patience. (Col. 3:12)

"Chosen . . . holy . . . beloved." Let these descriptions sink into your heart and mind, and consider what each word means.

Ask yourself: How does knowing that I am *chosen* mean I can be compassionate and humble? How does being called *holy* lead me to kindness? How might the awareness that I am loved result in patience and meekness?

3. Are there others you compare yourself to, thinking that your trouble is worse than theirs? Or is there someone you struggle to feel compassion toward? How can you change your attitude?

## Pray

*Dear Lord, you see me and know me, and I praise you for this, that you, the God of all the universe would pay attention to me. Help me to remember that I am not forgotten but am seen by your loving eyes. By your Holy Spirit's power, enable me to rest in this knowledge. Interrupt me when I dwell too much on my troubles, and turn my gaze back to you. Help me to notice other people, and extend your compassion to them. In Jesus's name, amen.*

3

# Step Out

### Forward with Jesus Is Always
### the Right Direction

*Lord, if it is you, command me to come to you.*

MATTHEW 14:28

SEAT BELTS, VITAMINS, BAG CHECKS.... Daily life is full of the precautions we take to protect ourselves. They are so common we rarely notice that they are there keeping us and our communities safe. And as technology develops, so more and more forms of self-protection appear, from antivirus software to vaccines.

Of course, we should protect ourselves from health threats and from those who would want to harm us. Still, constantly watching for danger can damage our hearts and minds. What starts as sensible self-protection can easily lead to fearfulness and self-preoccupation, limiting our willingness to take risks and look beyond ourselves. Again and again, we might see opportunities and say or think to ourselves, "No, thank you. I can't go out. I can't serve. I can't lead. It's not safe."

This might make us feel safe, but we end up being like a hibernating dormouse curled up, inert, and malnourished. In this short chapter, we are going to explore ways to overcome these urges to keep saying no by looking at Jesus's courage and the promises of God.

In Matthew 14, as we've already seen in the previous two chapters, Jesus acts bravely. He feeds five thousand people with just five loaves of bread and two fish (vv.15–21), and he walks on water (v. 25). Perhaps it looks to you as if these miraculous, extraordinary events are no sweat for Jesus. But consider that his divine knowledge was limited in the incarnation; he didn't know everything. Doesn't it seem brave to you, then, to organize a huge group of people for a picnic, when in your hands is barely enough for a couple? And to start walking onto (or would it feel like into?) a deep lake in the stormy dark? Both of these acts were a courageous choice to make himself vulnerable. Jesus could have done what his disciples suggested and sent the crowds away (v. 15), but he didn't. He could have waited until it was light and walked around the perimeter of the lake to meet his disciples, but he didn't. Jesus chose to do the difficult and the dangerous things, because he trusted in the Holy Spirit's power and his Father's word.

When I (Sarah) taught little children Bible stories a long time ago now, I used an old set of felt figures. The Jesus character was blond, and his clothes were a pristine white. Put him in any flannelgraph scene, and he stood out as different from the other felt figures, like an ad for laundry detergent. We know, though, that

Jesus didn't look different from other people (Isa. 53:2). He was a Middle Eastern man whose clothes got dirty just like everyone else's. He didn't just look the same, however. Jesus also experienced the same temptations. Just like you, Jesus felt the temptation to do the easier thing instead of relying on the Spirit's power and on his Father's word.

Perhaps you remember the time in the wilderness when Jesus was tried by Satan? There he was tempted to make bread and to throw himself in the way of danger (Matt. 4:1–7). Instead, he obeyed his Father's commands and did not do the miracles that Satan urged. He responded to Satan's challenges with Scripture. In these new challenges of crowds and storms, courageous obedience meant *doing* the miracles out of love. He chose to multiply bread and to walk on dangerous water because he cared for his people.

By remaining faithful to Scripture's commands and patterns, Jesus demonstrated courage. In providing a miraculous meal, he followed his Father's example. Again and again in the Old Testament, God had produced food for those who were hungry, first in the form of manna and quail for the Israelites in the wilderness (Exodus 16) and then for Elijah (1 Kings 17:2–16). He also provided for Ruth and Naomi (Ruth 2:17–18; 3:15) and for David (1 Sam. 25:18–20) through the providential generosity of others. What's more, in Isaiah 55, God called out "Listen diligently to me, and eat what is good, / and delight yourselves in rich food," connecting the image of free abundant food with his satisfying word and the promise of new life (v. 2). On the hillside, then, as Jesus taught and thanked God for the food before distributing it, he was not only obeying God but also fulfilling Scripture, showing himself to be the God who provides life-bringing bread. Even more amazingly, he was pointing to the truth that he himself is the bread of life (John 6:35).

When Jesus walks on water he is following his Father's pattern in a similar way. The Lord had overruled the waters of the Red Sea (Ex. 14:15–22) and the Jordan River (Josh. 3:14–17). He promised his people that when they "pass through the waters . . . they will not sweep over you" (Isa. 43:2 NIV) and is described as the one who stills the storm (Pss. 89:8–9; 107:28–29). Jesus shows that he is the powerful Lord, but he also acts as a vulnerable man—in fact, he acts as Israel, that very vulnerable nation of weak people. Jesus represents the people of God who should trust, take courage, and obey. Having taken on the form of the lowest kind of man, a servant, Christ humbled himself and obeyed (Phil. 2:6–8). This was the opposite of self-protection. Jesus trusted in his Father's power to protect him as he stepped out in faithful obedience.

In this, Jesus gives us not only an example to follow, but the source of the courage we all need to follow him. Peter cried, "Lord, if it is you, command me to come to you on the water" (Matt. 14:28). Peter was astonished at his Master on the sea, and longed to come out to meet him. Could he defy the water as Jesus did? This story isn't about how one man went to his local lake to break the laws of nature. It's about how we are supposed to fix our eyes on Jesus and trust in him totally, even when in our own strength we would sink. The Lord is for you and will uphold you, whatever your circumstances.

Lewis and I have known Nick for a number of years. We've watched him start out in his career, fall in love, and get married. Along the way, things haven't been easy. His job wasn't what he'd hoped, and the wife he loves was diagnosed with a physical disability. Nick has managed to keep going. Sometimes, though, he felt that people overwhelmed him with their needs, and so he simply avoided them. Helping his wife sort out the garden or gaming? The console often won. Going to his church discipleship group or TV and an early night? Easy to tell himself that he needed the extra rest. Nick wanted to protect himself from other people, so he avoided them. He wanted to avoid risk in his life, because he'd found that things that look exciting tended to cause trouble and that the demands of others could overwhelm him. Nick kept politely and persistently saying, "No, thank you."

Nick, however, is changing. He's begun to grasp the lessons of Matthew 14. He gets that Jesus isn't just a faraway example of someone doing hard and extraordinary things. He's the Lord who, because he obeyed God courageously, is able to protect and provide for his people now. Jesus is still able to deal with hunger and the storms. Philippians 2 tells us that because of his obedience, Christ is now "highly exalted" (v. 9) and is the source of "encouragement," "comfort," and "participation in the Spirit" (v. 1) for those who believe. He doesn't leave his people in danger and want; he rescues and shelters and nourishes.

Nick discovered that he didn't need to be always protecting himself from demands and danger. He could rely on Jesus to be with him, and he could get on with obedience. This slow change has started with switching his mantra of "No, thank you," to "I'll give it a go." The small steps of attending discipleship group regularly and serving at home are steps he can take because of his growing sense that Jesus is taking care of him. Jesus's care is for all of us and takes us forward in the right direction.

## Reflect

1. Take time now to meditate on Matthew 14:25–33.

Are there people or tasks that you are avoiding? Write a list of the four most significant ones (make sure that you're not including any jobs that are actually someone else's responsibility).

Out of this list, choose just one item to focus on. What is it about this person or task that makes them scary? What is it about yourself that makes you feel as though you can't do what you need to do here?

Take time to pray for a growing sense of God's presence and power to help you, and memorize Matthew 14:27: "Take courage; it is I. Don't be afraid" (NIV).

## Pray

*Lord Jesus, I thank you that you made yourself a vulnerable servant that you might bring power to those who trust in you. Thank you for not shrinking back from the challenges you faced, so that I might be given your courage. Please forgive me for the times when I try to protect myself and hide away from difficulty, ignoring the great protection and strength you offer. Please give me strength to keep asking you for your strength.*

*I pray this so that you might be glorified and so that I might love you more. Amen.*

PART 2

———

# YOU CAN STOP NOW!

If resilience is about keeping-on-going in the storms of life, why is there a part on stopping and resting so early in this book? Surely, that's all wrong! Perhaps you've picked up this book because you can't seem to get going at all or because you feel tempted to give up on what you are doing. Permission to stop might seem like a really bad idea, but actually, it is just what's needed if you are going to succeed in perseverance. Charlotte knows breaks are important, in fact she often feels exhausted and joyless, and longs for a rest, but there is far too much to do for her to stop!

She is on her feet much of the day at work, and when she gets home at night, she tries to study—she's taking extra training courses in her "free" time. Sharing a house with others means there are plenty of distractions though, and she often goes to bed later than planned. Weekends are more study, extra work shifts, cleaning the apartment, or visiting her relatives (which is sometimes more a chore than a pleasure). There's church as well, which means serving in the nursery or on the coffee rotation. Then it's Monday and work again.

It's all okay though, Charlotte reckons. People are made for work. Aren't they?

It's true that it's good to have a job, serve others, study, and reach out to people. The very first command given by God was "fill the earth and subdue it" (Gen. 1:28); people are to "rule over" all the other creatures that had been made (Gen. 1:26 NIV). That certainly sounds like hard work. The New Testament doesn't seem to change this emphasis; Paul tells servants, "Whatever you do, work heartily, as for the Lord and not for men" (Col. 3:23). It doesn't even stop there, because if we take seriously the pictures of heaven as a renewed earth, then work won't be abolished, just perfected.

It looks as though we humans are definitely made to work. And our Western culture seems to agree.

I (Sarah) was brought up on a farm where work rarely stopped. If we felt like taking a day off, there was no one else to step in and help. When I was growing up, the real heroes were those who stood on their own two feet and who knew how to work hard.

It's not just farming families that harbor attitudes like this. Many urban workplaces take it for granted that employees will go above and beyond their contracted hours, staying late or clocking in early.

All of this can give us some strange ideas of what it means to stop work to rest. It can make us feel guilty and unable to stop, or it can become an idol, something we long for, thinking it will set us free from the burden of work that we resent.

My friend Tom lives for the weekend. Hard work is just a means to an end for him. It provides the money he needs to fund his mountain-biking trips and holidays. If he can't go out, then it's computer games and take-out. He's busy chasing dreams of leisure, and church is just slotted in when there's nothing more exciting on the horizon. Perfect rest is a never-ending quest for Tom.

Neither Charlotte nor Tom have it right. We're not made to be defined by leisure or by work that leaves us drained. The good news is that the Bible paints a picture of rest which is far more exciting than we might expect. It starts with stopping, but it leads to remembering who we are and why we are. Rest brings us an opportunity to reorder our days and our hearts. Resting can even be painful, but it can also be a relief.

4

# One Day

## The Sunday Gift

*I will give you rest.*
MATTHEW 11:28

IT IS GOOD NEWS that the Bible speaks truth for both the work-focused and the leisure-seeking. King Solomon, who had a full life with all his wisdom gathering, ruling, and building, not to mention his (disastrously unwise) collection of wives, wrote this:

> It is in vain that you rise up early
>     and go late to rest,
> eating the bread of anxious toil;
>     for he gives to his beloved sleep. (Ps. 127:2)

Here are two kinds of life. There's the busy, busy, restless, stressful one, which Solomon says is "in vain," or pointless. The metaphor of "eating" here suggests that in this kind of highly-driven life, "anxious toil" is what feeds us. This isn't in the sense that our wages pay our grocery bills, but that work is what gives ultimate meaning. In this life, work has taken over everything.

The other kind of life in Psalm 127 isn't described by *doing*, instead the focus is on *receiving*; to these people God gives both love and sleep. "His beloved" are defined not by their work but by their relationship with him. Rest follows from that.

This is a challenge. My friend Charlotte (from the part 2 introduction) is a Christian, but she doesn't feel rested. She feels as though work rules her. And despite my friend Tom's searching for the ideal holiday, it is rarely the paradise he hankers for. He's just left feeling restless. Why should finding rest in all its forms seem so hard even for those who know Jesus loves them?

### The Creator's Rest

Perhaps we need to step back and see more of what the Bible says about rest. Move from Genesis 1 to Genesis 2. On the seventh day, once God had completed his creating work, he rested (Gen. 2:2–3). Stop there and marvel!

It is not as if the all-sufficient God should ever get tired or bored and need a break. His rest speaks rather of satisfaction and enjoyment in both the "very good-ness" of creation and in himself. It's as if on this one day of the week the curtain is pulled back, and we get a glimpse in time of the triune God's continuous, eternal self-delight.

This rest day shows us that God is more than a heavenly engine, mindlessly moving to keep the world going. God is personal.

He doesn't exist for the purpose of work, and, therefore, neither should we. He delights in what he has made and invites us, made in his image, to enter his delighting rest of real refreshment.

Rest isn't an afterthought. The seventh day is the climax to the story of creation, a day of completion that is blessed and made holy (Gen. 2:3). It becomes a priority in the cyclical pattern that God establishes, for individuals, communities, and even for the land itself, as later Sabbath regulations show us (see Deut. 5:12–15). As Jesus tells the Pharisees when they criticized him for picking grain on the Sabbath, this day is "made for man" (Mark 2:27; see also Matt. 12:1–14). Israel's Sabbath regulations were not made to be a burden. They were given so that people could be blessed and devote one day every week to joyful restoration. That's why Jesus taught and healed on the Sabbath. He was living out the real purpose of the Sabbath.

In the same breath as saying that the Sabbath is a gift for us, Jesus makes another, perhaps even more profound claim. He tells the Pharisees that "the Son of Man is Lord even of the Sabbath" (Mark 2:28 NIV). Jesus is saying here that Sabbath isn't merely a look back to creation or to the exodus, but that it is *his* day. For that reason, though the death and resurrection of Christ bring seismic change, a day of rest is no less important. Our rest day looks to the cross of Jesus, and it points ahead to his future return. We can even say that rest finds its significance in Jesus. Let me explain.

Throughout the history of Israel, God's people were promised rest, even though they already had the Sabbath. There was rest from enemies and rest in the land of milk and honey. They had tastes of it, but the rest never lasted. When Jesus came, however, true rest arrived.

Hebrews 4:9–10 tells us that "there remains, then, a Sabbath-rest for the people of God; for anyone who enters God's rest also rests from their works" (NIV). This means that rest isn't simply about not plowing your fields or some modern-day equivalent on a certain day or even about gathering to worship but about how we stand before God.

**The Savior's Rest**

The Sabbath was a symbol of humanity's need to set aside the exhausting work of trying to do things on their own or to be good enough for God. But this need is met in the work of Jesus on the cross. Sin alienates us all from God, making us restless and without peace now, and threatens to put us into a restless torment for eternity, separated from God. When Jesus says, "I will give you rest" (Matt. 11:28) he really is promising to bring us the peace of forgiveness we need, now and for eternity. He was restless on the cross—struggling and tormented, as he bore our sin, so that we might find peace from him in forgiveness for those sins. So God's command that we rest means that we rely on all that Christ has done and look forward to the rest-filled restoration of all things in him. To truly enjoy a Sabbath rest is to trust in Jesus and enjoy him.

**Remember the Sabbath?**

From the early days of the church, the Sabbath has been translated to the Lord's Day. It has moved from the last day of the week to the first, marking the shift of focus to Jesus's cross and resurrection. The promise of spiritual rest has been fulfilled, but the symbol of this rest, one day set apart, is there for Christians to enjoy.

Each Lord's Day is a fresh reminder of all that Jesus has done for us and a promise of what's to come. It's not about us! We set aside our independence, our self-absorption, and our racing around to get stuff done, so that we can remember Jesus and share in his act of re-creation as he builds his church.

This remembering takes place as we make clear choices about what we listen to, what we eat, what time we set our alarms, or what books we read. We might want to cook double the day before so as to avoid slaving over the stove on Sunday. We might need to work a bit harder at our jobs during the week to protect our resolve to not return until Monday. We might choose to listen to worship music, rather than the news, on the drive to church. We may even choose to limit our church duties if possible to approach worship with more focus.

We remember the Sabbath too as we consider what the impact of our choices will be on others. Will our actions help them find rest spiritually and physically too? Maybe you could invite someone to eat with you who would otherwise be alone, and certainly you can delay sending that email, so that someone else isn't caused to pick up their work on Sunday too. What about the needs in your neighborhood? Is there time on the Lord's Day to reach out with acts of kindness to people you know are finding life tough? There's real joy for us as we celebrate God's generosity by sharing it with others.

## Slow and Deliberate

Building a routine of making one day distinct like this as much as we can doesn't just have one day's worth of impact. Remembering our rest in Jesus on a Sunday can kick-start a week of remembering and rejoicing.

What might this look like for Charlotte and Tom? Could they take time, once a week, to stop rushing? Could Tom stop his restless pursuit of perfect leisure and could Charlotte say no to slogging away at her work and studies? Laying aside both the bucket list and the to-do list might be a start in helping them to remember all that Jesus has done.

For both Charlotte and Tom, slowing down on one day might mean really getting to know people in their churches, chatting after worship or over meals. They could slow down to pray in more detail. They could slow down to notice the world immediately around them, changing pace so that when Monday comes they can work with more energy and patience in the tasks that have been given to them by God, knowing that these things are important but so is real rest.

None of this is particularly sophisticated. In fact, it is deliberately simple. Sabbath rest is simple because at its heart is a celebration of what God has already done and is doing, rather than an attempt to perfect something new ourselves. Keeping things different on one day in the week, so that we can celebrate his work brings deep rest for the spirit, body, and mind.

## Reflect

1. What is your tendency, to idolize work or leisure? Take some time to meditate on these verses where David focuses on God as the one who brings him protection, hope, and rescue:

For God alone, O my soul, wait in silence,
    for my hope is from him.
He only is my rock and my salvation,

my fortress; I shall not be shaken.
On God rests my salvation and my glory;
   my mighty rock, my refuge is God. (Ps. 62:5–7)

2. What one or two small changes could you make in your week to make your Lord's Day a day of rejoicing in and remembering the Lord's rest?

3. The Sabbath wasn't the only time the Old Testament people of God took special time to remember God's grace. Three times a year they celebrated festivals together. How can you make sure your holidays are *holy*-days—times in which you can make extra space to rejoice in the gospel?

**Pray**

*I am sorry, Lord, that my mind is so often full of what I must do and so little filled with what you have done for me in your death and resurrection. Forgive me for rushing about seeking significance and pleasure in things that will not last when you have provided me with all I need.*

*Thank you for the precious gift of rest. Help me to see where I am restless, and give me grace to keep remembering you, which is true rest. Help me to form habits of slowing down that I might enjoy relationship with you and your people. Heavenly Father, by your Spirit strengthen and direct me through this, so that I may play my part in building your kingdom here on earth. In Jesus's name, amen.*

5

# Every Day

## The Rest That Restores

*He gives to his beloved sleep.*

PSALM 127:2

*. . . the cares of the world and
the deceitfulness of riches . . .*

MARK 4:19

THE LORD GIVES HIS BELOVED rest by giving them a rest day,
a gracious sign of his work for them. What about those other six
days? They can feel like a sprint or even an assault course, fast
paced and relentless, full of to-do lists and back-to-back trials.
But if Sundays form a rhythm for the week, there is a rhythm for
each day too, which starts with sleep.

## To Sleep

The created world has a rhythm. Genesis 1 establishes the pattern with its repeated refrain, "There was evening, and there was morning" (vv. 5, 8, 13, 19, 23, 31). The sun rises, and animals wake and birds sing; it sets, and they go to sleep. There is seedtime and harvest. While the technologies of modern, urban life might mean that we don't notice these natural patterns as easily, completely ignoring God-given circadian rhythms and staying awake through the night will do us physical harm and it might do us spiritual harm too.[3]

Back in Genesis 2, not long after we are told that God rested, we see the first-ever sleep.

God brings Adam into the garden "to work it and take care of it" (v. 15 NIV) then makes him fall asleep so that Eve might be created as his companion in this work that cannot be performed alone (vv. 21–22).

Imagine it. Adam is only just made and still perfect, but he is in need. The answer comes in this death-like state of sleep. Just like the Sabbath, which whispers to us of our need and God's grace, so sleep reminds us of our dependence. And while we sleep, God works to bring help.

## Sleep: God's Death and Resurrection Masterpiece

When you sleep, amazing things happen in your body and brain. Memories are sorted; the cardiovascular system slows down, reducing wear and tear; the hormonal system is rebooted. You don't need to understand the science, however, to understand how good sleep is. In the sixteenth century William Shakespeare wonderfully celebrated "the sleep that knits up the ravell'd sleeve of care," as if daytime anxieties pick us apart, but sleep mends us. Sleep is "sore labour's bath" and "balm of hurt minds."[4] He understood the restoration that a good night's sleep brings.

We can only really keep going in life if we sleep. And to fall asleep is, as Fred Sanders says, "a good opportunity to entrust yourself, your entire self, to God's care . . . to relinquish control to a God whom you have to trust."[5] When anyone sleeps, they demonstrate the reality that they can't do it all, that they are not in charge.

When your eyes close and you drift off, what happens is a kind of death. When you wake, you experience a resurrection. For Adam, this was more than metaphorical, because while he slept, he didn't just lose consciousness, he was broken open. And through his wound a new life was formed. He woke to meet his "bone of my bones," his bride, his Eve (Gen. 2:23).

I don't know if Adam's eyes were bleary when he awoke or whether he felt a bit dazed as he opened his eyes. What's certain is that, taking in the sight before his eyes, he was filled with joy (Gen. 2:23). Adam's life was renewed as he discovered the help that he and God's new world needed standing in front of him: this wonder-woman, Eve.

So sleep is necessary, not just physically and mentally but spiritually too. It teaches us our great neediness and limitations. It reminds us that we are frail, finite creatures. It shows us God's ability to renew and remake us. And it points to Christ, the one whose side (like Adam's) was wounded and who slept in death. It points us to the creation of Christ's bride, formed through his death and resurrection, for union with her Lord. What a gift of grace sleep is!

Therefore, when any of us awaken from our sleep, before our minds focus on the things we are (or aren't) looking forward to, we need to pause and pray. Thanksgiving at the end of the day is good; how about the beginning of the day, too? Can you thank God for the new life he has given you, for the mini-resurrection he has just performed in bringing you up from sleep? What about praising him that you are not alone in this new day with all its burdens, but that by the Spirit you are united to Christ and are part of his bride, the church? Rather than hitting snooze and rolling over, you can get up, because the Lord of the universe is with you.

### Grace for the Small Hours

What if, though, anxieties keep you from sleep or wake you up in the dark? What if you wake in the morning, but you can't pry your body out of bed? A desperate desire to sleep or frustration about sleepiness can sometimes make sleep even more difficult, as well as embittering.

When you feel powerless over your own body and unable to make yourself sleep, you need to embrace the truth that sleep and strength are gifts. Meet the fear that "I've only got four hours until the alarm goes off, I'll not cope with tomorrow's demands" with the Lord's promises to carry the weak (Isa. 40:11). Tomorrow will be okay because he is with you. Remember that God's grace is still strong and sufficient even when you are tired in your bones. Rather than thinking over the worries that look so much worse in the dark, trust each concern to the Lord. Those times of lost sleep are not wasted. Our prayers and our praises in the night are heard by the Lord who never sleeps.

So Christians can celebrate our Lord's nighttime care. Before we close our eyes, we can say to God (as David and Jesus both did), "into your hands I commit my spirit" (Ps. 31:5; Luke 23:46 NIV), consciously trusting ourselves to him who cares for us (1 Pet. 5:7). We can make it a habit to remember, as we lie down, that we belong to him and that he is our "good shepherd" (John 10:11) who "restores [our] soul" (Ps. 23:3).

## Prone to Wander

For some of us, though, perhaps for many of us, restless minds and hearts during the day are a bigger problem than sleeplessness at night. Having decided to move to a new house this year, I (Sarah) was reminded how difficult moving is. The physical labor of shifting boxes and lifting furniture is exhausting. On top of this physical strain, my mind had a hundred more things to be distracted by. As a family, we were literally "un-settled," being between two homes, and this led to feeling unsettled by a myriad of legal and financial tasks as well as labyrinths of domestic decisions requiring online research. Juggling so many questions meant that I had a mind and heart battle with restlessness.

This problem doesn't arise from a lack of health or cash. Sometimes restlessness arises precisely because we have so much, rather than not enough. We have so many choices, so much information, so many sources of entertainment and, from a global perspective, so much material wealth. Smartphones and laptops have brought this world of rich opportunity to our fingertips. Such abundance creates particular kinds of pressure and temptation. There's so much out there to be seen, listened to, or bought that we have barely begun to enjoy what we have before we're on to the next thing. Like the choking thorns in the parable of the sower, which represent the "worries of this life and the deceitfulness of wealth" (Matt. 13:22 NIV), the distractions of abundance are temptations that can stop our faith from producing the fruit of godliness.

Restlessness can come from other sources too. We all want things easy. In fact, we can be greedy for ease. We want instant pleasure—and we've got used to receiving it, in a way, from our smartphones. We rarely want difficult people or tedious work. Lack of concentration can be related to a lack of contentment in the circumstances the Lord has given us now. Or it can be a result of real difficulty that leads us to yearn for anything that will take our minds off our pain.

Whether we are bored because things are too easy, or we're sad and frustrated because they are too hard, discontent can make us wander, mentally and spiritually. Christians know that God should be their rest and joy, that he is the only one who brings real satisfaction, but how quickly we all look to immediate pleasures to fill us up!

## The Battle to Focus

The battle against distraction and restlessness begins, then, in the heart. Psalm 37 commands you to "delight yourself in the LORD" (v. 4). It is good to enjoy the gifts of work and leisure, but your first priority is to enjoy the Lord. When any of us fail to see Jesus as delightful, our minds drift and chase other distractions. This verse continues, "And he will give you the desires of your heart." Tasting the beauty and sweetness of our Lord transforms our desires. When we see how good he is, we want to know him, we want to please him, and we want to serve him. The stuff that often preoccupies us pales in comparison.

So there are two interconnected disciplines to pursue: (1) to look to Christ and (2) to look away from distractions. As we look to Jesus, we will be lifting our gaze from unnecessary stuff. Perhaps that sounds simple, but our plans and resolutions to be more self-controlled are usually very short-lived, whether they involve our phones or exercise or prayer. A few days or a week or two of trying to be disciplined, and we think we've got it nailed; but then a problem comes up, and we fall back into old habits. For the new practices of Christ-focus to stick, we must ask for his help. If we don't, then change won't come, because it's grace that brings lasting change. Can you pray, "Lord, help me to delight in you, transform my heart so that I might desire you more than distraction" not just once but every day?

Distraction-free focus is often called *flow* and is a state of mind that is especially creative and productive. Musicians are good examples of people who pursue and often excel in this kind of focused output. People doing practical tasks also can know such a deep immersion in what they are doing that they can lose sense of time. You might experience it when you are reading a book or watching a great film. In fact, what we love doing is often the place where we are least aware of the world outside our activity.

If restfulness is in part a habit, then building into our days opportunities for flow to happen can help train our brains to be better at concentration. This isn't an alternative to seeking to be with Christ but can be a way of enjoying the gifts he has given you in a way that honors him as well as a means of practicing restful focus. It might be that you have a hobby, or part of your job in which you can be fully absorbed. Maybe there is something new you could try, or something you used to do that you can go back to. I have a highly educated, Jesus-loving friend who loves sewing. She has found that making clothes and experimenting with textiles helps her to rest. Another friend tells me that when he is fishing his mind is fully focused and, though it is physically tiring, it brings mental refreshment.

Blocking out an hour or so each day in which you put away other distractions and focus on the one thing you have chosen to do is good for you. It can also help to get a grip on the rest of your time. Turning off or putting time limits on your phone; blocking websites that you keep turning to when you're bored; time-tabling your days so that there are clear and simple goals for each hour, rather than one endless and overwhelming to-do list, will all help. It is good to limit shopping and watching and email-checking, not because these things are wrong in themselves, but because seeking simplicity in life can help us all keep going with Jesus.

How does this work? As you put away distractions and work on your ability to concentrate, you can develop a simple life focused on Christ. Having a quiet time or devotional time each morning is an excellent practice (and your concentration on Scripture then might be better with more order in your life), but how about remembering his presence throughout the day?

If you can stop checking your phone while you are waiting for a bus or for the kettle to boil, can you start using those few moments to reflect on him? If you can strip away some of the unnecessary stuff that fills the day and your mind, maybe you can concentrate better on the essential things you are doing. Seeking radical contentment in Christ might mean you do each task deliberately and carefully, conscious that it is a good thing the Lord has given you to do. You can even give thanks to him for each opportunity. There is a deep restfulness in this mindful, grateful reliance upon the Lord, as you remove attention from unnecessary stuff or from yourself and give glory to him instead.

We love visiting our friends' beautiful home. Among the pictures on their walls is a metal plaque inscribed with these words: "Bidden or not bidden, God is present." It always makes me pause and think.

How good would it be if all of us were more conscious through the day of God's merciful presence by his Spirit? It's a truth that can motivate us to cut out distractions, and more than that, it can empower us to focus on what matters. God is present to help us. In relying on him and rejoicing in him, we can find rest every day, all through the day.

### Reflect

1. Do you long for sleep or resent having to sleep? If sleep is a profound way of entrusting ourselves to God, how should your attitude and habits around sleep change? Pray to the Lord about your ideas.

2. Do you want to desire and delight in Christ more? If so, ask the Lord to help you see more of his beauty and grace. Are there points in the day when you can take a moment to refocus your gaze upon him—perhaps the time when you are prone to be distracted. This week, make this a time to reflect on him—perhaps you could use

one of these verses? Write them out and place them somewhere visible so that your thoughts are drawn back to the Lord.

I am continually with you;
    you hold my right hand.
You guide me with your counsel,
    and afterward you will receive me to glory.
Whom have I in heaven but you?
    And there is nothing on earth that I desire besides you.
My flesh and my heart may fail,
    but God is the strength of my heart and my portion
        forever. (Ps. 73:23–26)

Awake, O sleeper,
    and arise from the dead,
and Christ will shine on you. (Eph. 5:14)

This verse from Ephesians is probably a quote from a song, and it is a call to repentance and faith, but it stands too as a call to wake up out of our sleep or our distractions and trust the Lord!

3. What could you do practically to put off distractions? Make a list of several changes and pick one to focus on this week.

## Pray

*Heavenly Father, forgive me that I forget so often that you are with me and for me. Thank you for the great gift of your Son in my place and the presence of your Spirit who opens my eyes to see your love. Lord, you know my heart. You know my frets and hurts and discontent. Please grant me the ability to trust you in the day and in the night. Give me the strength to stop and rest at night, and give me, please, the strength to focus each day knowing that you are with me and that you have work for me to do.*

*In Jesus's precious name, amen.*

PART 3

---

# HOPE-FULL

Change is possible. Hope is power. At least, that's what an ad for one of the UK's leading newspapers says. I'm not sure everyone would agree.

Take my friend Nadia for instance. She's bright and kind and creative and fun. But her hopes regularly come to nothing. Stuck in a tedious minimum-wage job with anti-social hours, she is desperate to branch out and do something far more interesting. So, she writes applications, sends them off, and waits. Sometimes she'll land an interview, and she'll start dreaming of her new life and planning her commute. She hopes and waits but nothing happens.

It's been like this for a couple of years. Interviewers leave her hanging, so after a few weeks she has to assume they don't want her. Then it's on to the next application: more hoping, more waiting. A vision of a brilliant future has kept her going, but now she's starting to wonder if it is all worth it, whether it is worth hoping for something more at all. She's getting bitter and disillusioned. As the writer of Proverbs puts it, "Hope deferred makes the heart sick" (13:12).

It's not as if Nadia wants a lot. She's a Christian. She prays and trusts that God is in charge, but continual rejection takes the wind out of her sails. You might be praying for a good thing as well. The conversion of a family member or self-control in your online habits. For healing of a long-term health condition or an end to your anxiety. You pray and hope, but your heart gets sick in the wait.

And, in that sickness, while words about God's love and Bible promises might be meaningful for others, they taste as dry as dust to you. Behind the sickness, resentment gnaws away—resentment at the people who don't change and at situations that never end and at the God who doesn't seem to act. How can you keep on hoping when even little glimmers of light keep being snuffed out?

Hope sometimes doesn't feel like power, it feels like foolishness. High hopes can lead to horrible hopelessness.

The Bible has something to say about that feeling, but it isn't a simple "cheer up!" or "be less optimistic!" or even a "wait for heaven!" No, the Bible's advice is far bolder—the apostle Paul would say, "Boast in your hope!" These words feel shocking! The next three chapters will help us to see how we can stand with such extraordinary confidence about the future.

# 6

# Those Who Hope in the Lord

## Fix Your Hope on Easter Truth

*Christ Jesus our hope.*

1 TIMOTHY 1:1

ONE OF NADIA'S PROBLEMS is that she's always looking forward but not very far ahead. She's looking in her email for an invitation to interview next week. Or she's daydreaming about a year's time when she's all settled in that new job and how great she'll feel then. Boasting in hope doesn't mean that she should hype up her hopes further. It means she needs to reconsider her hopes completely. That starts by looking back.

When I (Sarah), like Nadia, get disappointed and frustrated in my hopes, it's often because I've got my eyes on the wrong past. I think back to my college days and reckon that because they were good a great future lies ahead. Surely, it's what *should* happen. Or, with a rather clouded nostalgia, I remember all the friends I had when I was younger and expect that ahead of me is a brilliant social life. It *should* happen soon, right? I'll keep hoping because, really, I deserve some blessings soon. After all, as Miriam sang in *The Prince of Egypt*,

> Who knows what miracles,
> You can achieve,
> When you believe . . .[6]

Sometimes memories are troublesome in a different way. There are dark, shadowy memories, maybe of mistakes and failures; the times I spoke hasty words or stayed away from someone in need. The way I chose to do what I knew was wrong again and again. Or, perhaps worse, the way others failed and wounded me, the times when I was bullied or ignored or taken advantage of. Memories like these can choke hope, because they make us believe that God shows up for other people but not for us. In these instances, we might still talk optimistically about our dreams, but below the surface we think, "Good stuff shouldn't happen to me; I don't deserve it" or "He might promise big things, but those big things will bypass me. They usually do."

The problem with all this looking back, however, is that the past we often look to, whether dark or sunny, is not sure enough and not far back enough.

The apostle Paul would say, go back further. Look to what Jesus has already done for us. In Romans 4:25–5:2, just before he talks about boasting in our hope, he speaks to Christians about Jesus like this:

[He] was delivered up for our trespasses and raised for our justification. (v. 25)

You've maybe heard and said those words many, many times, but stop and reflect on them now. Two thousand years ago, Jesus accomplished two things for you if you're trusting in him. Out of two definite, completed actions, one in darkness and the other in the light of a new morning, come two wonderful realities.

Jesus's death was "for," that is, a *punishment* for our sins. He was punished for our anger and resentment and the way we justify ourselves but blame other people. He gave himself for our desire to have things our way and for our habit of putting ourselves first. His death paid for our endless lies to ourselves and others. His suffering was for our self-absorption and our reluctance to think about him. All our sins were dealt with and are completely forgiven. Those mistakes and failures are now like dark stains washed clean away. While my version of my own past is often out of focus and self-centered. God's is crystal clear; I deserved death, but on the cross he died for me.

Then, when all the punishment was done, Jesus rose from the dead. That's the second completed action.

In the church I grew up in, Good Friday was a big thing. It was very quiet and still, the building was emptied of everything that was colorful, and we seemed to sing very slow, very old hymns. I can't remember Easter Sunday services, though, and that's a very great shame. The cross was center stage, and Jesus's resurrection seemed to have been sidelined. But look how important Easter Sunday is in this verse. It tells us that Jesus was "raised for our justification" (v. 25). The Father raising the Son from the dead by the Holy Spirit is the greatest miracle. Death, which ends every human life, was overpowered. Paul connects this with God's declaring us righteous. We're not only washed clean of sin, but we are also dressed in Jesus's perfect life. His obedience becomes ours. His victory over sin becomes ours.

## This Past Never Fades

Paul doesn't stop there; there are more benefits flowing from the first Easter:

> Therefore, since we have been justified by faith, we have peace with God through our Lord Jesus Christ. Through him we have also obtained access by faith into this grace in which we stand. (Rom. 5:1–2)

These past events are not just something to look back over and feel emotional about, like old, faded family photos. Instead, they make an ongoing difference to the present.

Believing that Jesus has died and been raised for you is a bit like moving house. He's picked you up, given you faith by his Spirit, and put you in a brand-new home. You once lived in a war zone, a rebel fighting back against God's love and lordship. Now you're in a place of peace. The house you now live in runs on the rule of grace. Because Jesus died and rose again, you are safe here; God is for you. You "have been justified"; you "have obtained access" to his grace. It has been done: you are now and forever at peace.

This all means that our hope is based not on future projections—what might happen—but on the certain, definite past. That's why we can boast in our hope.

What's more, the coming of Christ and the victory of his cross is itself an example, perhaps the one greatest example, of long-held hopes which have been gloriously fulfilled.

Think about Isaiah looking ahead, wondering and waiting, yearning to see the shepherd king he'd preached about who would rescue Israel; or Micah, in such turbulent years for the nation, asking when this king would come out of Bethlehem. These men and so many others hoped and hoped. But they too were looking back, their hope was based on God's work and words in the past.

Isaiah called Israel to,

> Look to the rock from which you were cut. . .
> look to Abraham, your father,
>    and to Sarah who gave you birth. (Isa. 51:1–2 NIV)

The prophets were remembering covenant promises God had made to Israel's forefathers. They were remembering God's work in the exodus, rescuing a people for himself from slavery. And because of this certain history they could look forward. God wonderfully fulfilled their hopes, so now we can look backward and see that, yes, God does do what he promises. He has *already* done what he promised.

So, if he's done this, kept his promises in such an extraordinarily generous way, by lavishing his love on us in giving Jesus to die for us, then keeping the rest of his promises is a small thing for him. If he's done this, as Paul reasons in Romans 8:32, then will he not continue to do you good, to "graciously give [you] all things"? Remember, you're living in that new house, the house of grace. Clinging to this truth, above all else, is the way to survive and even thrive in the Christian life.

So how can Nadia not shrivel up because of defeated hopes? How can you learn resilience? The answer is to look to the incarnation of Christ and see there the loving Father's overwhelming commitment to your good. We can all look to the cross and see our guilt acknowledged and cancelled. And we look to the resurrection and discover God's victory over death by his Spirit. That is why the apostle Paul, the man who endured so much discouragement, danger, and suffering, could speak of the Savior as "Christ Jesus our hope" (1 Tim. 1:1). He truly is.

This is where all true hope really starts. It isn't that hope itself is power, as the newspaper wants us to believe, but true, Christian hope is hope *in* power, in the power of the Father's faithfulness, in Jesus's righteous life and death, and in the Holy Spirit's effectiveness now. Trust him.

### Reflect

1. What disappointed hopes have you experienced? What hopes do you still have for the near and longer-term future?

2. What are some of the failures or achievements you look back to that shape your hopes for the future?

3. This week, find a time each day when you can reflect on the cross. It need only be a few minutes to be focused and helpful. A friend of mine does this in the shower every morning. As the water rushes over her, she remembers her sin and the cleansing that Jesus has brought. It's a time for her to thank God and delight in the incredible generosity of his love. Others do it first thing when they wake up, when the to-do list or the reminders of things not achieved threaten to seep in. How about you? Look back and give thanks, building your hope on what Christ has achieved.

## Pray

*Loving heavenly Father, you know my heart, my longings and hopes and disappointments. Thank you that in the midst of these I can find solid ground in your grace by faith. Help me to keep looking back to the cross and the empty tomb, and to keep boasting in your love for me. When I am tempted to shape my hopes on what I think I'm owed, remind me of your undeserved love and keep me praising you.*

*All for Jesus's glory, amen.*

# 7

# The Hope of Heaven

## Glory Is Waiting for Us

*We rejoice in hope of the glory of God.*

ROMANS 5:2

IF YOU FIRST NEED to look back for resilient faith, you still can look forward. Your gaze needs to lift beyond interviews and romance and children and holidays and even the furthest pension plans to heaven itself, to the "hope of the glory of God" (Rom. 5:2).

Do you sometimes struggle with that idea? I do. I (Sarah) fear that if I were to talk about heaven at work all my colleagues would think I'm weird. If I talk about heaven to my children they come up with questions like "What will we eat?" or "How old will I be in heaven?" which I can't answer. So I often end up avoiding talking and even thinking about heaven, suspecting that heaven might actually be weird and confusing and just too remote to be worth considering.

## Jesus, Heaven's Glorious Hope

Paul's words help me here. It is "the glory of God" Christians are to hope for. These are words that speak of a reality we can begin to grasp, because throughout Scripture, the glory of God refers to his overwhelmingly beautiful presence. On Sinai, as the Ten Commandments were given to Moses, there was fire and darkness and a loud voice so that the people feared for their lives and said, "The LORD our God has shown us his glory" (Deut. 5:24). When Solomon dedicated the temple, it was filled with "the glory of the LORD" and he fell amazed on his face (2 Chron. 7:1, 3). Hundreds of years later, when Ezekiel was with a bedraggled group of exiles far, far away from that temple, God showed him an overwhelming "appearance of the likeness of the glory of the LORD," and Ezekiel fell down in worship (Ezek. 1:28).

You haven't seen any dazzling lights or heard a thunderous voice, but if you've met Jesus in the pages of the New Testament then you've encountered God's glory. You've seen displayed his holy beauty, which is "the radiance of God's glory and the exact representation of his being" (Heb. 1:3 NIV), "full of grace and truth" (John 1:14). In Scripture, you've heard him speak tenderly to an excluded woman drawing water at a well. You've watched him reaching out to a beggar covered with sores. You've seen him forgive those who were tasked with his execution, and draw close to his doubting disciples after rising from the dead.

Christians are not so much hoping for a place or a time. We're hoping for a person. Our hope for the glory of God is a hope to see Christ in all his fullness, the wounded and reigning Lamb. As the old hymn says,

> I will not gaze at glory
> But on my King of grace;
> Not at the crown He giveth,
> But on His pierced hand;
> The Lamb is all the glory
> Of Immanuel's land.[7]

One of the wonderful things about this kind of further-off hope is that it holds together all that we can know about eternity. There's justice here, because Jesus is in charge. There's comfort, for he's promised to wipe away every tear. There's community because, as the bridegroom, he must have his bride, which is the church—the numberless crowd of people from every tribe, nation, and tongue. And there's beauty and meaning in the worship that surrounds him, full of the story of grace.

### Secure in Our Hope

Back to Nadia. As she hopes for a job that will really fit her gifts, her eyes are on an ideal future, or at least a better future than her present. We've all been in that kind of situation. Perhaps you're in it now, daydreaming of an "if-only," hankering after an opportunity that will give you wings and lift you above the gray everyday, or longing for a respite from pain that has made you sore for what seems like an age. Maybe it is even a hope that your ministry in church will become much more fruitful, with, of course, fewer wrenches thrown into the works by your coworkers. Getting a right perspective on Christ as our eternal future brings a clear light in which we can evaluate these short-term hopes.

When we consider the utter security of our future hope, that our names are written in the Lord's book of life, we can see our little, shorter-term hopes for what they are—uncertain and, even if fulfilled, temporary.

We all come to the end of a career at some point, however impressive it is; health eventually fades; the best of friends disappoint, and Christian ministry and serving will never reach a stress-free stage. None of these truths are bad news; in fact, they are liberating. Knowing that our human hopes are so frail allows us to rest rather than exhaust ourselves trying to build a perfect resume, body, lifestyle, or church. Four hundred years ago, Thomas Brooks knew this reality but found that future hope was the best comfort. He wrote, "Hope will keep the heart both from aching and breaking, from fainting and sinking; . . . hope is a beam of God, a spark of glory, and . . . nothing shall extinguish it till the soul be filled with glory."[8] Our kingdoms will not come. Jesus's kingdom will.

I'm always taken aback by Jesus's words to his disciples who came to him breathlessly joyful from their first mission trip. He acknowledged that all they had done had been his gift and reiterated his promise that they were safe, but he warned, "Do not rejoice that the spirits submit to you, but rejoice that your names are written in heaven" (Luke 10:20 NIV). Just at the moment when they expected a celebration of past success, Jesus gently and firmly put the focus on future security. Using a present tense imperative, he showed that this certainty is something we must delight in now. The plans for his kingdom have been completed, the eternal outcome is secure.

So as we delight in the certain hope that we will see our resurrected, living Lord, we can sift our smaller hopes. It's not wrong to have hopes for our earthly futures. But perhaps we need to check that they work with our biggest hope.

Do your hopes for the here and now match with your eternal hope? If you're hoping for a new job, why is that? If you're hoping for a change of scenery, why? What lies behind your hopes for more money or for the salvation of a relative or for harmony in your church family? So often, if we are honest, we realize we want these good things so that, at least in part, we might have an easy life or feel better about ourselves. Our hopes for next week, next year, or ten years' time could be disconnected from, maybe even clash with, our great hope. We must seek to align our hopes in this life with the greatest hope of heaven.

Your secure future hope is rooted in Christ and looks toward him, if you are a Christian. So look at him now. You may still want a job, marriage, money, or peace, but as you hope for these things, look for Christ in them. Can you hope for opportunities to serve, be fruitful, and give? Can you hope that he would be glorified in all you do? Those are hopes that will surely be fulfilled.

### Reflect

1. Is heaven often in your thoughts? Make it a point this week to thank God every day for the certainty of glory ahead.

2. Reflect on these words from Revelation 7:17, focusing on the centrality of Christ in heaven and the particular promises of his care here:

The Lamb in the midst of the throne will be their shepherd,
and he will guide them to springs of living water.

3. Make a list of your day-to-day and longer-term hopes. What are you really longing for through these? Is it comfort and significance? Bring them to the Lord, asking that he would orient these smaller hopes toward his glory.

## Pray

*Dear loving Lord, I want to praise you because you have set before me (a frail and fallen human being) the hope of seeing you as you are in eternal glory. Help me to take this blessing in. Please change my thoughts and attitudes through the certain knowledge that I will spend eternity worshiping you. Forgive me that I so often hide from this fact and hope that I would be glorified instead. Please make me wise and generous in how I hope now. Amen.*

8

# Hope Today

## Living with the Hope of Glory

*Christt in you, the hope of glory.*

COLOSSIANS 1:27

WITH ALL THIS LOOKING BACK and then looking forward, while also keeping an honest realism about the difficulties of life, you might be beginning to think that we just need to grin and bear the present. Don't fear—that's certainly not the case! Hope isn't just for the future or focused on the past. In the New Testament, hope is a transforming force for the present, springing from the indwelling of the Holy Spirit.

In Colossians 1:27, Paul writes about a mystery that has been unveiled, which is "Christ in you, the hope of glory." This means that hope isn't something we manufacture in ourselves by furrowing our brows, straining our eyes, and concentrating ever so hard. The hope of glory has been given to us, if we belong to Christ.

## The Hope-Filling Spirit

We are connected to the past triumph of the cross and our future glorification through "God's love [which] has been poured out into our hearts through the Holy Spirit" (Rom. 5:5). This love, Paul says, is the reason why "hope does not put us to shame" (v. 5). This hope isn't a flimsy IOU note, a messy scrawl with a vague promise of payment. It is a live, present, active hope. Christ, who conquered death and won for us an eternal hope, lives in us.

But there is a catch.

The passage from Romans 5 ties hope to the Holy Spirit but also to suffering. Paul writes, "We rejoice in our sufferings, knowing that suffering produces endurance, and endurance produces character, and character produces hope" (vv. 3–4).

Does that sting? If the ground for our hope is Christ's peace-bringing death and victorious resurrection, the way we experience hopefulness is through suffering. This topsy-turvy truth seems like the opposite of what we thought about at the beginning of this part. We might feel as though hardship wears away our sense of hope, like waves that break day by day on a cliff, sometimes eroding the surface minutely, sometimes bringing about a sudden rockfall. Instead, Paul says that these waves can expose and polish hope.

Even our best hopes are often laid on false foundations. We might hope that our churches will grow but are pinning our hopes on great preaching and skillful musicians. We might hope that our friends will convert to Christianity, but we're actually trusting in our own activities and apologetic skills. We might hope that we won't go back to viewing porn, but we're hoping in software and accountability structures.

As we suffer, whether through waves of outright persecution or in the ongoing and wearying difficulties of life, the inadequacy of those foundations is revealed. When external structures let us down, and we can't maintain our relentless activity, we are caused to depend on Christ's resources not our own.

Day by day, the question comes, will you trust in his strength to fight sin? Will you forge self-denying habits that speak of dependence rather than success? This is the kind of endurance that Paul is talking about here. It is these battles and the armor we need for them that we'll be exploring together in the chapters ahead.

But for now, know this: out of perseverance and growth in grace come changed character. When we lived in London, there were three older women in our church family. Each of them had been abandoned by a husband decades earlier in an age when divorce and single-parenthood were seen as deeply shameful. This had brought them poverty as well as emotional suffering. They were all very different personalities. Harriet was a thoughtful booklover, interested in ideas; Fran was no-nonsense and very practical, ready to speak her mind; and Jane was always rather quiet and shy. Their personalities were all different, and they were certainly not perfect saints, but each woman had the character Paul talks about, honed by the Holy Spirit through suffering.

Harriet, Fran, and Jane all showed the Spirit's fruit of love, joy, peace, patience, kindness, gentleness, faithfulness, goodness, and self-control in the ongoing grief they suffered (Gal. 5:22–23). Fran had lost the hope of being a grandmother. She and Harriet had also lost the hope of a materially comfortable old age, and all three had lost the hope of a companionable marriage and the status it would bring. But "character produces hope" (Rom. 5:4). As their characters were changed by daily experience of the Spirit's power, enabling them to say no to bitterness and despair, so they experienced a welling up of hope. Everyone saw it and took heart.

Jesus said, "Whoever believes in me, as the Scripture has said, 'Out of his heart will flow rivers of living water,'" and John interprets this for us: "Now this he said about the Spirit" (John 7:38–39). When talking to the Samaritan woman, who, like Fran, Harriet, and Jane, knew shame and probably abandonment, Jesus said, "The water that I will give [the believer] will become in him a spring of water welling up to eternal life" (John 4:14). These beautiful pictures of the Holy Spirit as living water bring us wonderful assurance.

### Real Hope, Lasting Change

You don't need to screw up your heart to try to be hopeful or search in your circumstances for any tiny positive signs to cling to—he said this or she did that. Instead, because the Holy Spirit is alive, he can keep on and will keep on renewing and refreshing you like a mountain stream. Your hope is in his power to keep you going through life, to bring new life to others, and to resurrect us all for eternal life, just as he resurrected Jesus on the first Easter morning. And so, just as we all hope in his power, so his power renews our hope. When you delight in the present reality of hope and fight to keep on believing, hopefulness will bubble up.

I (Sarah) started this part with Nadia's story of employment frustration and her loss of hope. Her story isn't finished. Life for Nadia hasn't become radically easier or her work more interesting. I chose to tell you about her, though, because her hope has grown.

As her perspective has gradually shifted from career-breaks to Christ and his people, there is a new peace about her. Her habits have changed. She has a greater hope of heaven, which allows her to live more fully in the present. She's seen opportunities she didn't know existed to serve others in her job, which is, of course, still hard and menial. Suffering, for her, has produced perseverance, and her character is growing. As she endures through tough stuff, hope has begun to blossom—hope in God's present power, not in her career advancement. Change is possible, because hope is God's powerful gift.

**Reflect**

1. Think of a difficult situation you are facing at the moment. In this situation, what are you hoping for, and where does your hope come from?

2. How are you tempted to not persevere in difficult situations? What practical steps could you take so that you keep on going? What can you commit to pray to begin this process?

3. Why not commit Romans 5:1–5 to memory this week? Break it down into short sections and take your time. Even if you feel dry and hopeless, speaking the truth to yourself helps.

## Pray

*Father, thank you that you have poured out your living water, the Holy Spirit, into my heart, to change me into the likeness of your wonderful Son. Strengthen me to persevere in the situations that seem so hard right now. As I cling to you, change my character, and by the power of your Spirit, please renew my hope. In Jesus's name, amen.*

PART 4

---

# BODY LIFE

During Covid-19 UK lockdowns, we had nearly eighteen months of online church. Almost all worship services, prayer meetings, Bible studies, and pastoral sessions were conducted through screens. It was better than not meeting, but it was very different from (and far, far worse than) meeting in person.

There were no baptisms and no Lord's Suppers. No opportunity to hold the hand of someone in pain or to embrace those who were celebrating. Not even a chance to sit in silence and weep with the recently bereaved. It was hard to engage with sermons when sitting on a sofa and, to be properly honest, through a small laptop screen. If we didn't know it before, we know now that spiritual life isn't separate from bodily life. We have been created to listen, to see, to touch, and to be with others. Virtual life isn't a substitute.

The truth is that your body, mind, and spirit are interconnected. Nancy Pearcey tells us that each person is an "integrated psycho-physical unity."[9] This means that the "real you" is not a spiritual or mental being, which happens to be hidden in a disposable suit of flesh. Nor are you only a bundle of cells and electrical impulses. You really are body, spirit, and mind wonderfully woven together (Ps. 139:13–16).

Christians should know this already, of course. The gospel connects physical events with spiritual reality. We are vulnerable and complex creatures who depend, body and soul, heart and mind, on a great heavenly Father. Our sin is physical and spiritual, and it has spiritual and physical consequences, in both judgment and salvation. The second person of the Trinity, the Word of the Father, took on flesh. He ate and drank, remembered and reasoned, laughed, wept, and prayed. He died on the cross and rose again—body, mind, and soul. And one day, we'll join him with resurrection bodies.

This all means that we need to pay attention to the different dimensions of our beings. There's no area that is outside of God's interest or influence. There is a spiritual dimension to what we do with our bodies, and there's a physical dimension to our spiritual experiences. These next two sections will explore food, exercise, and work as examples of how to think through the significance of everyday action, and through them, we will learn how building strength in these areas of life will help us endure in the faith with resilience.

# 9

# Appetite

Bringing Our Habits and Desires to Jesus

*He satisfies the longing soul,*
*and the hungry soul he fills with good things.*
PSALM 107:9

IN THE EIGHTEENTH CENTURY, more British sailors were killed by scurvy than by warfare or accidents. In one voyage, 1300 out of 2000 men died of this horrible disease. The antidote was simple: consume vitamin C. This was well understood by some sea captains and doctors, but tragically the knowledge wasn't acted upon. Those who knew were too selfish or too absorbed with other, seemingly more important, concerns to ensure the welfare of those sailors in their care.

We've come a long way since then, but even now we still neglect what we know is good for us with serious results. Like those sea captains, we can be focused on important, even exciting, business but ignore what we do with our bodies. Our culture is awash with good advice about physical health, but many of us, Christian and non-Christian alike, struggle to put it into practice.

In this chapter, we're first going to consider eating and then exercise, two areas where we can easily feel like failures. Diet and exercise stand as examples of other bodily aspects of life that can be both blessings and snares. Maybe for you, instead of eating, sex, or spending brings particular heartache, or it could be something as mundane as ordering your home. Together we'll seek to answer why these habits are so prone to induce shame, pride, or joy and see what God's word has to say about our bodily struggles.

## Spiritually Hungry

Part of the answer is that physical appetites are bound up with heart desires. Just like the Israelites in the wilderness who fantasized about cucumbers, pomegranates, pots of meat, and onions, we often fixate on certain foods when life is tough (see Num. 11:5). We're rightly hungry for food and celebratory shared meals, but we're also hungry for comfort, hungry for control, and sometimes hungry for distraction from pain. The pressures of poverty, stress, and distress and society's obsession with cooking shows and diet regimes contribute to eating problems, but these external forces only exacerbate the hunger problems already hiding in our hearts.

This is delicate territory. There's a great deal of pain tied up in issues of diet. A well-intentioned comment about food can shatter confidence and relationships. But this, like other areas of appetite, is something we mustn't shy away from. The Bible certainly doesn't.

When Paul warns us to avoid "greed, which is idolatry" (Col. 3:5 NIV; see also Eph. 5:5 NIV) and to beware of those whose "god is their belly" (Phil. 3:19), he is talking about worldly desires or "desires of the flesh" in John's language (1 John 2:16). These desires supplant a right desire for God—and they include our appetites around food. These desires aren't necessarily about piled-up plates or a sugar addiction—they could just as well be a desire to control the intake of food through excessive calorie counting or purging.[10]

In a world that often seems chaotic or disappointing, food can be a god that brings us immediate comfort and satisfaction, and we think we can control it. Turning to the cookie jar again and again when we are frustrated or chasing the perfect diet can mean that, instead of us controlling food, our appetites end up controlling us. When we put food first, we worship an idol that cannot save but surely destroys. Bad eating—in all its manifestations—leaves us tired, weak, isolated, sometimes ill, and often angry with ourselves. God's wisdom on food, thankfully, is good medicine for us all.

## Food That Satisfies

Eating has a massive place in the story of the Bible, not as an incidental detail, but as a more-than-symbolic figure. In the garden, Adam and Eve were provided with an abundance of good fruit to eat and a particular fruit that would bring life (Gen. 2:9). But once they chose the wrong fruit, eating came under a shadow. Food is cultivated with trouble (ask any farmer or cook), and consumption falls short of the satisfaction and communion it promises.

Yet, through the Old and New Testaments, we see God provide abundantly and miraculously for his people again and again, climaxing ultimately in Christ, the bread of life, broken for us. Just as he did in Eden, God provides food so that his people will learn to trust him as they wait for the promised future banquet. We now live in the overlap of the difficulties of eating and the climax of God's free feast. Knowing this can help guide us through our eating issues.

## Enjoying God's Feast

We can start with the simple fact that because God has given us living bread to eat—bread that lasts to eternal life—and keeps on lovingly providing daily bread for us as well, we don't need to eat to excess whether out of habit or in distress. Knowing that we are accepted and loved and that he is in control of the uncertainties around us means that we don't have to control our intake of food excessively either. The comfort of his love can help us to say to ourselves, "Stop—that's enough!"

So often when we're eating for the wrong reasons, we eat quickly, almost mechanically. Remembering that food is a special gift from the Lord for our good can help us to slow down and savor mouthfuls. The tradition of "saying grace," perhaps even if you're only snacking or eating on your own, is an excellent way to reflect on the goodness of God. In that moment you can remember it is the Lord who truly satisfies. The food you're given, whether it's chicken wings or tomato salad, is a sign of his great love for you to be received with gratitude and, very often, shared.

Problematic eating is so often something done in secret and kept there. By sharing food when we can, we help each other. Our out-of-kilter desires can be restrained simply by the presence of our brothers and sisters, who create a new context and meaning for eating. The old expression, "breaking bread together," with its echoes of the Lord's Supper, illustrates this idea. A simple meal unites the people who share it. Sit round a table with others to eat, and your independence is limited. When passing the salt or the potatoes, we eat what we're given or share what we have. We're reminded that eating is about more than personal choice or preference, it's about gifts and relationships.

When Jesus teaches us to pray "Give us this day our daily bread" (Matt. 6:11), he helps us to get the right perspective on food. It is a gift from our loving Father, which makes it important for us, but also it doesn't last—so we need to ask for it each day. What's more is that this request for daily bread in the Lord's Prayer is sandwiched between requests for God's kingdom to come and for his forgiveness to be experienced. Food isn't an end in itself; food is part of the world ruled by God and the world needing his grace. It is an often delightful and always necessary fuel for a life of godly dependence.

## Running the Race

Living this life of trust and obedience isn't easy, of course. It takes focus and discipline, and it might be tempting to think that although we all definitely need food, we don't really need exercise. Going to the gym might seem like an option for those keen on sports or even a vanity project for those worrying about their figures. But that's not true. Paying the right kind of attention to your body is spiritually healthy. And we'll see, exercise doesn't just strengthen muscles, it strengthens emotional and mental resilience as well.

When the apostle Paul told Timothy that "physical training is of some value, but godliness has value for all things" (1 Tim. 4:8 NIV), he was not minimizing the value of exercise, but setting it in proper context. Active devotion to God, he is saying, is significant in all parts of life, always, everywhere. But training your body is still important! If physical training had some value in New Testament times, when manual labor was a necessary part of life for most people, how much more value does it have now, when work for many of us often involves just sitting behind a screen? We must take seriously the "some value" of physical training!

It is hard to overstate the difference that exercise can make to our mental and emotional, as well as physical, well-being. Hormonal highs are well known, but there's also an increase in brain activity, which promotes nerve-cell growth for long-term improvement in mood regulation. When so much of modern human existence is lived virtually, through smartphones and laptop screens, putting the body through its paces, ideally outside, can help us remember what is real. A brisk walk or running up some stairs quite literally grounds us. Exercise teaches us that the body is more than a suit the "real me" inhabits. You are formed by God: body, soul, and mind fused together.

**Valuable Play**

Christians in Sport, an organization that encourages discipleship and witness in the world of sports, states on its website that we are all "born to play."[11] This is a helpful message for naturally competitive people who are driven by the thought of winning.

It's great to push ourselves and to improve, but all sport is play. It's a gift to enjoy. Through it, we enjoy the gift of our bodies, our health, and our relationships with others.

View exercise as play that is creative, relational, and free, and you may find the prospect of training more appealing. It stops being all about you and your goals. We remember too, that when children play they are practicing, in a safe way, the really important stuff of life. Play might involve losing, as well as winning, strategizing and taking risks, cooperating with others, following the captain's lead, and keeping to time. It is also fun!

Training our bodies, therefore, doesn't have to mean straining for ever tougher goals in pursuit of bettering ourselves or always beating others, but it does mean that there is often some discomfort on the way to progress. I (Sarah) enjoy running, but sometimes I don't want to leave the house. It might be raining or too hot or too cold. And I know that in the first ten minutes, I'll really want to stop. After pushing past those inclinations, I'm invariably glad I've been out. As I go beyond my natural desire to be easy on myself, I'm getting the "some value" that Paul talks about.

Of course, there's no automatic transfer of self-control or endurance from one area of life to another. Some top-class athletes have little sexual self-discipline after all. It depends on the heart's desires. But if you do desire to honor God, then training in self-denial physically is of use spiritually. Having to persevere up a hill in the rain might be much, much easier than continually forgiving someone who has wronged me, but it still reminds my heart that enduring tough things is possible. Pushing myself out of the door to run can also help me push myself to pray or serve or sing praise. Getting used to enduring physically can help us to keep going spiritually. As we honor God with this precious gift of a body, we honor him with our hearts too.

## Body Conscious

Exercise isn't just brain medicine or perseverance training. Getting up out of a chair and raising your heart rate can develop an increased awareness of your body, of yourself as a physical being with limitations, as well as your strengths. This is good for the soul. As we feel a stretch, or notice a sweat breaking and persevere (or take a break!), we remember that we aren't mini-gods but needy creatures.

What I'm talking about here isn't the kind of body-consciousness that comes from looking long in the mirror or even the body-positivity of pop culture, which insists you must celebrate your shape. Those are self-oriented, and so often they result in either pride or despair. Right awareness of our bodies as we walk or lift weights or simply sit, should, in contrast, make us more oriented toward our heavenly Father as the giver of this amazing, complex gift. He has knit each person together in a mysterious beauty: muscles, tendons, skin, and bones. He has even provided the very air that animates us every moment.

The Bible is full of the language of breath.[12] In Genesis 2:7, God breathes into Adam's nostrils to give him life. Much later, the risen Jesus breathes on his disciples, and they receive the Holy Spirit (John 20:22), who brings new life. Being aware of our physical breathing can lead us to trust in his ongoing provision of life and the safety of depending on such a great Lord.

And, if he provides every breath we breathe and knows and numbers every hair on our heads, then who are we to despise or dismiss our bodies? Instead, we should be grateful for them.

Of course, some of us will never have what others view as "fit" bodies because of serious health conditions and disabilities. Your physical training might be about persevering through daily discomfort or seeking to maintain some mobility. You may well feel that your body is more a burden than a gift, and your body-consciousness might involve a real awareness of pain. Most of us will also, at some point in our lives, share that experience as our bodies begin to age. What is certain, though, is the hope all Christian believers have for glorious resurrection bodies to be enjoyed when pain and disorder have finally been destroyed. If your body isn't functioning well or if, on the other hand, you are longing for a perfect physique right now, remember that real physical wholeness awaits you in heaven.

## The Best Body

Underpinning all this is the fact that Christ became a man. He depended on his Father for each breath. His body grew and aged. He ate and drank, feasted and fasted. He had appetites and formed habits of body discipline. He reached out to touch lepers, and he welcomed children with open arms. Jesus felt the burden of carrying heavy wood and then the excruciating pain of thorns and nails. He thirsted on the cross. He breathed his last. God, who cannot suffer, became man so that, as man, he might experience suffering for you. His body was raised, so that your body might also be raised.

When we wrestle with our appetites, wanting too much of something that is good, we can come back to the Lord Jesus and ask for his help. He who learned obedience through suffering (Heb. 5:8) is ready to listen and to help. He can help us deal with our unruly desires by transforming them, causing us to long to know him and be like him. He can help us use the gifts of food and exercise, which seem so ordinary, to glorify him in a beautiful, everyday obedience.

## Reflect

1. How do you usually view your body and its appetites? As a gift or as a source of shame or as a difficulty? How has this attitude shaped your habits around food and exercise or other aspects of your body-life?

2. Is there one habit you could adopt this week that will help you become more conscious of your body and its needs as a gift of God? Look back over the chapter to find some ideas.

3. Spend time meditating on this verse, where Paul calls us to lay out our whole self to God in worship:

    I appeal to you therefore, brothers, by the mercies of God, to present your bodies as a living sacrifice, holy and acceptable to God, which is your spiritual worship. (Rom. 12:1)

## Pray

*Lord, I thank you that I am fearfully and wonderfully made, that you have intricately knitted together my body. Thank you for the pleasure of movement and of food. Please forgive me when I neglect or misuse these gifts. Help me to grow in self-control and self-understanding, that I might persevere in the life you've given me. I look to Jesus, and I marvel at the way he was embodied, the way he ate and drank, slept and walked. Grant me grace to reach out to others and to share your gifts with them, using the energy you have given me. Amen.*

10

# Body Work

## How Everything We Do Matters to God

*Whatever you do, work heartily,*
*as for the Lord and not for men.*

COLOSSIANS 3:23

FLORA IS AN ART STUDENT. At her church she loves gathering for worship and enjoys teaching kids in Sunday school, but often feels out of place. If trusting and obeying God are the most important things, and if understanding Scripture is central, should she be spending her time making stuff with her hands or taking part in seminars about post-modern art and culture?

In the young adults' group there are some teachers, a builder, two trainee engineers, a midwife, and a few who are administrators. They all seem to have a clear view of how their work fits with being a Christian. They explain that they are helping other people and making money that can be given away, and they all talk excitedly about opportunities to speak about Jesus with their colleagues. Flora's experiences, working in a studio, just don't seem to fit. She wants to know whether any of her chosen career matters to God, or if it is all a waste of time.

## Garden Work

The questions Flora is asking are important for all of us. Many of us spend hours each day in an environment that feels a very long way away from church. You might even feel as though you have two identities: your working self and your Christian self. You might not work in the arts, you could be a journalist or work in IT or be a hairdresser, but you still might be feeling that you are split in two.

Living like this is never easy, and for some Christians, it means that they stop growing. All their emotional and mental energy goes into their careers, and their faith remains at the infant level. Then there are others who view their work as meaningless and just see their workplace as a venue for telling their colleagues about how great Jesus is. Of course, those colleagues rarely listen because their workmate pays so little attention to work and often does such a bad job. Finally, there are a few for whom the strain of having two identities means they just can't keep going as Christians, and they give up altogether. As you can see, our questions about work really do matter.

To answer these work questions, we need to go back to the garden again and see God's call for Adam and Eve in Genesis 1. They are to "fill the earth and subdue it, and have dominion over . . . every living thing" (Gen. 1:28). God has already shaped his creation, by ordering and naming it (vv. 4–5, 7–10) and then filled this universe with stars, plants, and creatures (vv. 11, 14, 24). Now people must imitate him, bringing order and fullness in his world. Theologians call this the cultural mandate. Not only must Adam and Eve cultivate the ground and domesticate animals to feed themselves; they also have to form a society. It is a command to creativity, hard work, skill, and sociability.

This first couple is to begin filling the world through pro*creation* but they are also to fill the world with things that must be imagined and designed and crafted. There's a need for pots and pans, houses and clothes. There's also a need for language and music, for farming systems and family routines. All of this is culture creation.

So we can't draw a line between imaginative activity (which some might see as dreamy and impractical) and the hard, physical work of everyday life. Scottish artist Alistair Gordon describes art as "a way of thinking or making sense of the world around us. . . . We respond to the ideas of our times."[13] Adam and Eve had to make sense of the world God had put them in. They needed to understand it and respond to it. When Adam named the animals, he looked, understood, and responded. As Christians we are all called to understand and then to respond rightly and creatively to God's scarred but still sacred world.

This might make sense to you but feel very far from your experiences at the moment. Work can be something you just survive or may be very temporary. Some of us are stuck behind screens or dealing with difficult clients or bosses. Perhaps you're surrounded by colleagues who are cruel or crass. Technology and the size of many of the organizations means that some of us feel like a small cog in a ginormous machine. Your skills or insights might not seem to count for much, and your hard work doesn't appear to get you (or anyone else) very far. In this fallen work, we're out of the garden and in the thistles and thorns. Labor can feel very messy indeed.

## Good Work

When work seems fruitless and frustrating, understanding more of the Lord's vision for work can help us keep going. Perhaps you remember the story of Mary and Martha (Luke 10:38–42)? Mary was sitting listening to Jesus, while Martha became flustered preparing a meal, and asked, rather resentfully, "Do you not care that my sister has left me to serve alone? Tell her then to help me" (v. 40).

Martha's annoyance is obvious here, and perhaps you've also said, "Don't you care?" to our Lord when your work is awful. The disciples asked this question of Jesus too, as they labored to control a boat in a furious storm (Mark 4:38). Work is hard and sometimes even scary in our fallen world, and we want Jesus's help.

There's not much immediate comfort here, however. In fact, Jesus's response could sound more like a telling-off. He said to Martha that there is only one essential thing, and that Mary had chosen it. He didn't get up to help, and he didn't tell Mary to either.

The necessary thing—that's for Mary and Martha and all of us—is to listen to him. This puts several things into perspective. When you feel overwhelmed or bored at work, you need to make sure you're turning to Jesus. "This is the work of God, that you believe in him whom he has sent" (John 6:29). Making sure you keep your focus on him will help you survive and will bring him glory. He is the center of the universe; your workplace isn't.

Because listening to and following Jesus is the one really important thing, we can all hold on to the fact that absolutely everything else is secondary. There's no hierarchy with pastors at the top followed by descending ranks of doctors, teachers, cleaners, artists, and at the bottom, the unemployed. If you're listening to Jesus and obeying him, then all activities can be worthy callings, whether you are paid or not, whether it is fulfilling or not, and whatever value the world puts on your role. What you do with your hours matters, however messy and frustrating it might be. You can find dignity and purpose in even the most frustrating and seemingly fruitless situations in life.

There's a freedom here, in this vision of equal work, and there's a narrowing too. We often think of paid work as superior and the stuff at home—hobbies and housework included—as inferior. But all can be part of this culture-building we're called to. When you're preparing a meal, as Martha was, or teaching a class, or stacking supermarket shelves, or dealing with a customer complaint, you are obeying the call to fill and rule the world God has made. Bringing order, beauty, love, and care in any situation is our service of the Lord.

Our labors are ultimately to honor the Lord himself. "Whatever you do, work heartily, as for the Lord and not for men, knowing that from the Lord you will receive the inheritance as your reward. You are serving the Lord Christ" (Col. 3:23–24). Even if no one sees or values what you do, if your heart is set on his pleasure, he is glorified, and he will reward. Rest secure in that confidence—and press on!

This work can be simply anything good, however menial. Perhaps it is worth asking if your workplace is somewhere you can love God and your neighbor. Are the aims and atmosphere of the business or institution making a good contribution to culture or not?

There's a phrase in Paul's letter to Titus which is repeated multiple times. Christians are to devote themselves to doing "what is good" (Titus 1:8; 2:3, 7, 14; 3:1, 8, 14 NIV). This is the opposite of "idleness," which Paul suggests can lead to gossiping and believing untruths about God and about other people.

I came across an old proverb recently, which goes: "Time on your hands, yourself on your mind." This fits what Paul is saying. When we're at a loose end, our thoughts can so easily circle around ourselves. When we do this, we can end up distorting our view of what's true and real, and we can do damage to others as well as ourselves. Doing good, on the other hand, is associated with being productive. It can be transformative to know that what we are doing is good and part of God's plan for the world.

I (Sarah) can give thanks for my work as a gift of God, rather than resenting it. I can aim to find ways of doing my work really well so that the good is multiplied, rather than skimping on effort, and doing things poorly. In the dull, repetitive bits, or the times when my boss has asked me to do something that just doesn't make much sense to me, I can pray for God's strength to do even these things with a consciousness of God's call to devote myself to what is good in the little space he's given me. And outside of paid work, I can bring a little more order and beauty to my neighbor's world through my home, hobbies, or various forms of service.

Working hard with our bodies, minds, and imaginations is a great privilege. In it we're imitating our generous Father who created and fills the world. Wonderfully, we can labor with light hearts, if we're first doing the one work he requires, which is to "believe in him whom he has sent" (John 6:29).

### Reflect

1. Make a list of all the things you are grateful for in the work that you do—whether paid or unpaid. In what ways are you creating and ordering in your work?

2. Consider these verses from Colossians and examine your heart. In what ways, in your daily toil, are you consciously serving the Lord? How might you need to change your attitude? Ask for his help to do this.

   Whatever you do, work heartily, as for the Lord and not for men, knowing that from the Lord you will receive the inheritance as your reward. You are serving the Lord Christ. (Col. 3:23–24)

3. What is one productive thing you could undertake in your leisure time this week that will bring blessing to someone else?

## Pray

*Heavenly Father, thank you for working to this day, sustaining the world through the Lord Jesus Christ. Forgive me for the times when I resent having to work or deal with a mess. Help me to commit to the great work of seeking you, and as I trust in you, give me strength by your Holy Spirit to do the work you've put in front of me wholeheartedly. Amen.*

PART 5

# THE RESILIENT GOSPEL

*Be strong in the Lord,*
*and in the strength of his might.*

EPHESIANS 6:10

The Bible is full of commands. If we don't heed them, and put them into practice, we simply will not stand in the battle, and be standing at the last day. Resilient Christians are those who hear God's word and do what it says, day in, day out. But hear this: it's not ultimately down to us. If we think that discipleship is all about our efforts, we will fail as disciples. There is far better news for us to live by.

It is the gospel that is truly resilient. The gospel stands, when everything else we want to cling to crumbles and disappoints. The gospel stands when we crumble, broken by our fears and failures, bitterly disappointed by life, and perhaps by ourselves most of all.

The gospel is always, always wonderfully true. It outshines the things that distract us. It outlives our seasons of struggle, doubt, or despair. The gospel never fails, and as we rest in God's gospel grace, neither will we.

The gospel is God's enduring and powerful truth. In the gospel there is real substance and real strength. The substance of the gospel is all about the Savior who has loved us and given himself for us, rescuing us from all that we are utterly powerless to escape from ourselves. He died, he rose, and he reigns for us, and exercises all of his power to protect us in his love before we enter the heavenly home he has prepared for us. When he comes for us—be it at death or at his second coming before we die—we shall know without a doubt that we have been saved by the gospel alone. God has invested the strength of his love and his power into the gospel. To believe is to experience this.

In this part we're looking at three parts of the Christian's armor, the helmet of salvation, the shield of faith, and the breastplate of righteousness (Eph. 6:14, 16–17). The apostle Paul gives his pen picture of the Christian dressed in spiritual armor in order to show us all we have in the gospel of Christ, so that we will be active in believing and living out our faith. Piece by piece, whether the defensive or offensive parts of the equipment, Paul shows us just how God has provided his full and final salvation in Jesus Christ. For all of our weakness, God has given us the strength of his powerful love. We'll learn how the gospel delivers us from fear and worry, and empowers us to be people of courage (the helmet of salvation). After that we'll discover how we can stand when temptation attacks, when we fix our trust completely on God's grace in Christ (the shield of faith). Finally, we celebrate how the gospel is the message we can and must always come back to, gladly swapping our failings for Jesus's perfect and conditions-free righteousness (the breastplate of righteousness).

11

# The Courage of Grace

## Think, Feel, Fight

*O Lord, my Lord, the strength of my salvation,*
*you have covered my head in the day of battle.*

PSALM 140:7

IN THIS CHAPTER we're exploring further the core message of the gospel. We simply cannot and will not stand in the Christian life if we are not convinced of how totally secure we are in Christ. The gospel alone brings us to God and sets us in his secure love. So let's look and learn about all that God in Christ has done for us.

If you're a young adult and you ride a bicycle, the chances are that you have always worn a helmet—or, at least, your mom or dad always nagged you to. The temptation to ditch the helmet is strong, though, isn't it? You like the wind in your hair and the freedom of jumping on and off your bike without having to remember a helmet or carry it around. A helmet just seems like a hassle, doesn't it? It doesn't really feel necessary, especially if you've cycled for hundreds or maybe thousands of hours without a single episode where it saved you. We have two children who might be brain-injured or even dead, if it weren't for bicycle helmets. One of our sons was strapped into his seat as a toddler when Sarah's bike did a complete flip, and he landed head first on the pavement. Another son went skidding across the road on a blind corner, and the bicycle helmet cracked on impact with a stone wall. They both hate wearing helmets, but helmets are the reason our sons are healthy and alive today.

Protect your head. If you're going to live a confident and a courageous Christian life, that means taking the greatest care of how you understand and think about your salvation. Paul says that believers must wear "the helmet of salvation" (Eph. 6:17). The helmet is critical armor. A bare-headed soldier won't last any time in conflict. Just so, Satan wants to throw you down, and make you forget your salvation, or lose confidence in it by allowing other thoughts to crowd your mind and crowd out your awareness of God's grace. But you must protect the way you think about your salvation. Only then can you live the Christian life well and live it courageously.

### Think Clearly . . .

Jim is a friend who struggles with anxiety over money, relationships, work, and health especially. When he was younger, Jim used to joke about his tendency to worry. Worry was like a muscle-reflex, an unconscious response to almost everything. Jim even got worried when he couldn't think of anything immediate to worry about! When he became a Christian, Jim's anxiety didn't float away, but it became something he now had the resources in Christ to deal with. So do we. We must take up the helmet of salvation, which means filling our minds with an awareness of God's truth and grace. When anxiety or any form of intrusive thoughts start to overwhelm you, you need to bring your mind back to the Bible certainties that speak a clearer, infinitely better message than the whispers of worry or fear.

A key verse for Christian living is Romans 12:2: "Do not conform to the pattern of this world, but be transformed by the renewing of your mind" (NIV). Our calling is therefore to allow Scripture to shape how we think, so that our renewed thinking leads to transformation of our feelings, our desires, and our living.

There's no magic switch for Jim (or for any of us) to turn off anxiety or any of our other temptations. The deliverance from a life of worry comes as we fill our minds with the promises and perspectives of the Bible, and the Spirit ministers them deeply to us. We learn to think differently, and Spirit-led thinking brings hope, comfort, and change. Authentic Christian growth always comes from a strong grasp of Christian truth.

The famous question and answer below from the Heidelberg Catechism bring the thrilling reassurances of God's gospel love. I suggest you read them out loud and take a moment to allow their truths to impact you.

Q. What is your only comfort in life and death?

A. That I am not my own, but belong with body and soul, both in life and in death, to my faithful Savior Jesus Christ. He has fully paid for all my sins with his precious blood, and has set me free from all the power of the devil. He also preserves me in such a way that without the will of my heavenly Father not a hair can fall from my head; indeed, all things must work together for my salvation. Therefore, by his Holy Spirit he also assures me of eternal life and makes me heartily willing and ready from now on to live for him.[14]

This is the gospel. Jesus has given himself for you and gives himself continually for you. Set his gospel-love in your mind and allow it to transform you.

### . . . and Live Bravely

As our minds are renewed, we are ready for the fight of faith. Battles aren't for the cowardly. We need to be brave. Wonderfully, being brave isn't about having a certain character, and it's certainly not about enjoying conflict. Bravery comes when we believe that certain things are so important that we must live in their light even when it means walking into difficulties. Christians who wear the helmet of salvation, filling their minds with Scripture, discover that its truths are so glorious that they can't help living them out. Courage isn't a feeling; it's about discovering God's help for consistent discipleship.

Do you hear much about our need to be brave as Christians, taking up our cross in embracing risk and opposition for the sake of Christ? I don't. Too often, we just decide what success might look like for us and pursue that, while avoiding the hard calls in the Christian life. In eternity, though, who will look back on their fleeting, earthly success when they've been too cowardly to follow the Lord and have any pleasure in it? Maybe we've got our notions of success and failure all wrong?

The legendary US baseball coach John Wooden liked to say, "Success is never final, failure is never fatal. It's courage that counts."[15] Think about it for a moment. Success, when you get it in life, is wonderful. You love it, and you want to capture that thrill and live with it for a long, long time. But success is deceptive and can breed complacency and pride. How many top business people or sports stars have got to the top of the profession only to come crashing down? Maybe they thought they didn't need to put in any effort anymore or that the rules of life didn't apply to them. A host of once-successful characters in the Bible are God's warning to us of the same danger. Success can breed terrible arrogance. They discovered that success, although so sweet, was not final.

Success is never final. Mercifully, when failure engulfs us, it needn't be fatal. Not, at least, in the economy of God's grace. Christ became a "failure" in the eyes of the world when he died alone, naked and mocked, for failures like us. Failure is the one connecting thread that draws each of us together, though we so hate to admit it. We are failures. That is the one thing we can be certain about each other: failure is written through us carefully covered over, explained away, airbrushed out of how we talk about ourselves. Our failure is undeniably there and sometimes glaringly obvious. Wonderfully, failure never defines us—Jesus's success for us does.

Coach Wooden is right: it is courage that counts. Courage to believe in Jesus and to take a stand for him. That doesn't mean actually feeling brave. Courage is action, not emotion. We can go into each day with an overwhelming sense of our doubts. We can speak for Jesus with a trembling voice. Discipleship with sweaty palms and crashing hearts as we step out for Jesus is still true discipleship. Discipleship when you feel scared but do the right thing for Jesus's sake is courageous discipleship. That's what counts. That's success. For that we must put on the helmet of salvation every day in a conscious, deliberate act. Then we stand brave and firm in the fight. And all this is because, in the words of the coach, "There is only one kind of life that truly wins, and that is the one that places faith in the hands of the Savior."[16]

"O LORD, my Lord, the strength of my salvation,
   you have covered my head in the day of battle." (Ps. 140:7)

### Reflect

1. What are some of your temptations at the moment (anxiety, pride, laziness, or something else)? How does the helmet of salvation "cover"?

2. Read the Heidelberg Catechism question and answer again. What surprises you and encourages you there? And what difference will it make?

## Pray

*Lord, help me to never forget that I follow a Savior and Lord who said no to every single earthly version of success. Please show me where the world is whispering its lies to me and where I am listening to them. Deepen my confidence in your word, and let your Spirit shape my thoughts as I read it. Make me a brave and loyal servant of Jesus. Amen.*

# 12

# Facing the Enemy

## Our Tempter and Our Shield

*Take up the shield of faith.*

EPHESIANS 6:16

WHY DO WE NEED a shield to live the Christian life? The Bible is clear: because we have an enemy, who is poised ready to attack us. He is the enemy who never stops. Ignore him or refuse to believe in him, and the result will be the same—acute danger. So says the apostle Paul, take up the shield of faith *in all circumstances* (see Eph. 6:16). We have been warned!

This chapter is about the gospel and temptation. Satan fires the arrows of temptation at us, and we find in our hearts that the seeds of temptation are already there. How do we recognize temptation? And what does it mean to lift the shield of faith and fight back, confident in God's gospel love for us?

In Ephesians 6, Paul likely has the Roman legionary's shield in his mind's eye. That shield had smashed the resistance of peoples from the north of England down to the south of Egypt and had brought millions under the control of Rome. At two and a half feet wide and four feet tall, this shield was the perfected design of layers of wood and leather, studded with iron and often soaked in water before battles to repel the enemy's burning arrows. Every person in the Roman Empire knew the sight of that shield. They might have hated it, but they knew that without it, there would be no empire. It worked. We Christians need the shield of faith, because we can't protect ourselves by our own efforts. We can't hide, but we can defend ourselves through faith.

When the Bible says that "the whole world lies in the power of the evil one" (1 John 5:19), it's not calling us to despair, but it is snapping us out of our delusion that the devil is at best non-existent or, at worst, the harmless memory of a bygone age. The prayer Jesus teaches his followers, "Deliver us from the evil one" (Matt. 6:13 NIV), still applies today. Through Christ we have decisively overcome him (1 John 2:13–14), but we need to still treat him as a powerful foe who can still harm us and purposes to. The shield of faith is the way we will keep the devil in his place.

## Lead Us Not

Why is temptation so hard to withstand? It's because it comes from the tempter himself, the devil who knows exactly what he's doing. He doesn't fire random shots in our general direction. No, he looks for our weak points, the gaps in our armor. He knows where to aim, and he knows just what temptations to send. Our temptations are unique to our characters, life-stages, past histories, and future longings, and they will change as we grow older too.

Temptations burn, just like flaming arrows. They can pierce us and set our lives on fire.

Some temptations come on suddenly and without warning. And with temptation, size is irrelevant. A third of London was destroyed in the Great Fire of 1666 by a few hot ashes from a baker's oven. Rising global temperatures lead to terrible wildfires in every continent. All of them start with a tiny spark. Just so, the smallest temptations can lead to the biggest sins, which burn with devastating impact.

Often, our temptations don't even seem to make any sense. They are illogical, but can bring catastrophe. We've all seen politicians or media celebrities who've been caught and exposed for something they've done, tearfully confessing their shame at a sin whose power over them they can't even explain. Temptation doesn't need to make sense to us for it to be a real threat.

Others burn more silently and sometimes aren't even noticed. Like an undetected health condition working away without anyone knowing it, some of our biggest temptations may be growing unseen in our hearts. They might be ambition, pride, discontentment, or ingratitude. They're all so hard to identify. Even when we suspect that they're there, we want to wave them away. We tell ourselves that we're imagining things or that we're dealing with little problems—not anything to get worried about or respond to. Often, our temptation is to tell ourselves that we have no temptation.

What undealt-with temptation might burn you? We need to have the courage to look closely at what our temptations are.

Here's a challenge: take an hour to be alone with the Lord, with your Bible, a pen, and paper. Pray and think. Ask the Lord to give you insight. Then write down the temptation points in your life. Maybe you can do it in twenty minutes or perhaps the Lord will open your eyes more gradually. But make a start! And as you realize what temptations you're experiencing, write them down, and make them a focus in daily prayer.

Recognizing temptation is the beginning of the battle. We must know our enemy before we can fight him. We won't make any progress unless we understand that specific temptations all have the same root temptation—unbelief. Whether we are tempted to pride or to despair, lurking beneath them all is the great temptation that Adam and Eve (and all sinners like them) faced: to refuse to believe that God is God.

How so? If we despair that our lives have any significance, we forget that it is God who gives us value. When we are puffed up with a delusion of our own glory, we refuse to believe that God is truly and alone glorious. As we nurse a vengeful spirit, we fail to trust that God is the righteous judge. When we play with sexually impure thoughts or give in to their drives, we refuse to believe that Christ has redeemed our bodies as well as our thought lives for his own possession. Temptation takes root where we allow the seeds of faith to wither. This is why we need the shield of faith, because only believing in the promises of God will deliver us from danger.

## Raise Your Faith

When temptation comes, faith must meet it. "Fight the good fight of the faith" (1 Tim. 6:12) is not a call to exercise some broad religious optimism. It is a command to meet temptation with the promises of *the* faith, the promises of the gospel of Jesus Christ. When temptation tries to take our hearts, either by storm or by stealth, the gospel calls us back to embrace Jesus as our deliverer. We cannot beat temptation by strength of will or by a new set of habits alone. We need Jesus. He is powerfully with us and for us as we actively trust him in the heat of temptation.

Believing means having a confident faith in a good God, revealed in his good word. He is good to us always, and we must trust that he is always good even when we're desperate. The French Reformer John Calvin defined faith as "a firm and certain knowledge of God's benevolence [meaning, his goodness] toward us, founded upon the truth of the freely given promise of Christ, both revealed to our minds and sealed upon our hearts through the Holy Spirit."[17] Even if you don't feel that God is good in that moment of temptation, Spirit-gifted faith goes to battle, certain that he actually is. The more we trust in his perfect goodness, whatever the situation, the more we learn to mistrust the lies of temptation. When sin wants to stick to us, instead we stick with Jesus!

This good God has given us a whole book of promises. J. I. Packer defined faith as "an object-oriented response, shaped by that which is trusted, namely God himself, God's promises, and Jesus Christ, all as set forth in the Scriptures."[18]

Faith can only operate when it's responding to what God says.

Every word of God proves true;
    he is a shield to those who take refuge in him. (Prov. 30:5)

Whatever temptation, whatever assault we face from the devil, we can be sure that, with the shield of faith, we have what it takes to stand. It is this shield alone "with which you can extinguish all the flaming darts of the evil one" (Eph. 6:16).

## Our Stunning Savior

Believing is looking. Looking steadily at what the Bible teaches us about Christ increases faith. This is the life of faith: "Looking to Jesus, the founder and perfecter of our faith" (Heb. 12:2). So let's look!

Look at him, so tender toward all who were beaten-down. *He was the bruised reed, bruised for you.*

Look at him, always accepting all who rely on him. *He was cast out, that you might be welcomed.*

Look at his cross and his empty tomb. *He died in shame and rose in glory for you.*

Look at his defeat of the devil. *He conquered him, for you.*

Look at his reign and the promise of his return. *He is ruling and coming back for you.*

Look at his promise to never leave nor forsake you. *He walks beside you.*

Look at his delight in believers. *He rejoices in you.*

It's all thrillingly, gorgeously true! May the Lord open our eyes more widely to Jesus and help us to raise the shield of faith as we rely on all that he is to us.

## Reflect

1. What have you learned in this section about temptation?

2. Go back to Calvin's and Packer's definitions of Christian faith. Does anything particularly strike you in those quotes? Are you totally sure of the goodness and trustworthiness of God (which are the foundations of true faith)? Speak to the Lord about this.

3. Is looking at Jesus—unhurriedly, intentionally, and lingeringly over his mighty acts for you—part of your regular worship? If not, could you start to build this habit into your time with the Lord?

### Pray

*Lord, show me Jesus. I obsess about myself, and I so easily miss my glorious Lord. Set him before me when I feel weak and tempted. Help me to fight, knowing that he fights with me and for me. Amen.*

## 13

# Battle Lines

### Confident in Jesus's Righteousness

*He put on righteousness as his breastplate.*
ISAIAH 59:17 NIV

OF THE VARIOUS PIECES of armor in Ephesians 6, it's the breast-plate that is the most important. For the Roman soldier this was a covering for the whole torso, leaving no vital organs in harm's way. This breastplate offered perfect protection. It also has the most fitting parallel in the gospel's protection that we're given in Christ. As we get to appreciate this gospel armor, we discover that it's the true and reliable protection we really need.

### Shiny, Unhappy People?

Do you ever catch yourself thinking that life's success is all down to you? You secretly fear that it's down to your efforts and your ability to solve problems, fight temptation, believe, be brave, keep going. No wonder the life of faith can feel bleak! You don't have the resources in yourself to do it. Nor do any of us.

We all try to get through life trusting in our resources though. We all wear armor. We wear it because we need to. One way or another, life is hard for every single person. If we open ourselves up to people, we get hurt. If we put effort into work or study, we may fail. If we speak up, we may get silenced. Some of us don't like how we look, behave, or sound. We all feel naked and inadequate, and we want to cover up. We already protect ourselves in so many ways, even if we've not yet realized it. We might be wearing the wrong armor, though. What are some of the wrong pieces of armor we could be relying on?

*The armor of laughter.* They've got a smile on their faces all the time and a quip or a joke for every situation. Others smile and laugh along with them, but they've really got no clue who the person they're laughing with is. Actually, it's because those armed with laughter are frightened to show who they really are. They give others a smile, but never themselves.

*The armor of criticism.* Others hide behind the armor of criticism. No one is ever good enough, nothing ever really comes up to their standards. The more they criticize others, the more they're trying to deflect criticism from themselves.

*The armor of moodiness.* Some prefer the silent criticism of moodiness. It's powerful armor, because everyone creeps carefully around them. No one ever gets close to the moody person in work or in church. They're the master of their relationships—but they hold everyone at a distance.

*The armor of avoidance.* Some are avoiders. They are very skilled at avoiding commitments, relationships, and all of the difficulties such things bring. Avoiding people and responsibilities (and their challenges), allows them to stay as they are, untouched. Lonely but untouched.

*The armor of busyness.* Some just love to be busy all the time. Maybe it makes them feel important. Certainly, it keeps others at arm's length. It even appears to keep God himself at a safe distance. Busyness protects them from thinking, from giving of themselves, and from being genuinely available to others except as their busyness dictates.

The thing about wearing the wrong armor is that, sooner or later, it will fail. Exhaustion, loneliness, fearfulness—the very things you tried to guard against—will show that your armor doesn't work. It might shine for a while and convince you and others that you're okay, but it doesn't work long term. In massive contrast, God calls us to throw all of our self-made armor away. Scary, maybe, but totally liberating. In its place, he offers us once-for-all protection through Jesus.

Jesus has all of the resources we need for living. He has already decisively fought every single one of our battles for us. By his Spirit in us, he is fighting those battles we face today. He keeps going with us, so we will endure. If we understand this, we will never think that our discipleship rests on our shoulders, and we will follow Jesus with hope and confidence. That is the true Christian life that we're called to enjoy.

## The Battle Belongs to the Lord

What does it mean, to say that Jesus has already fought all of our battles and will fight daily for us? It's the declaration that Jesus has decisively conquered all of the sins that separated us from God when he died and rose again. We failed to obey, but Jesus perfectly obeyed his Father for us (Rom. 5:18–19). We are now reconciled to God, chosen, made holy in Christ, and dearly loved (Col. 1:22; 3:12). He has conquered for us! The same conqueror now indwells us by his Spirit and fights with us by his Spirit.

So a Savior who is a warrior? That is the great promise of Scripture. Adam and Eve in the garden were told that one would come who would crush their enemy, Satan (Gen. 3:15). There are two places in the book of Isaiah where this promise of a warrior is especially clear.

First, in Isaiah 42, God speaks to his people when they were on the point of despair. They were facing defeat, with no hope. God gave them this stunning promise:

> The LORD goes out like a mighty man,
>     like a man of war he stirs up his zeal;
> he cries out, he shouts aloud,
>     he shows himself mighty against his foes. (Isa. 42:13)

God himself would shout a war cry as he came to fight for his people. They couldn't fight; he said that he would. Add to that a later passage, in Isaiah 59, which is an incredible promise for the same fearful people:

> The LORD saw it, and it displeased him
>     that there was no justice.
> He saw that there was no man,
>     and wondered that there was no one to intercede;

then his own arm brought him salvation,
    and his righteousness upheld him.
He put on righteousness as a breastplate,
    and a helmet of salvation on his head;
he put on garments of vengeance for clothing,
    and wrapped himself in zeal as a cloak. (Isa. 59:15–17)

What is God doing? Isaiah says that he's coming to rescue. Now take that promise of a coming warrior and see Jesus. See him fighting all the way to the cross, obeying where we have failed, resisting temptation where we've given in to it. Then see him gaining the decisive victory over our sin and judgment at the cross, where he paid for all of our wrongdoing. In life and in death he fights for justice, with a heart burning for zeal for his Father's glory, and for the salvation of his people. And his shout is the only victory cry we ever need to hear! "It is finished" (John 19:30). Our sin has been defeated by our warrior Savior. He has done it!

So Jesus has conquered our sin. What he has done—defeating sin to the glory of God—he now calls us to do in our lives with his Spirit's power. For this, we need to be secure in the awareness of his victory and access his power for the battle.

### Essential Battle Dress

Let's return to Ephesians 6, where we're commanded to "put on the breastplate of righteousness" (v. 14). What is this breastplate? And whose is it anyway?

First, it is Jesus's breastplate that we must wear. He has won our victory as we've been reminded. If we try to "wear" our righteous acts by fixating on how we're doing, we'll soon despair. We will be reminded of how unrighteous we are in ourselves. If we are wearing Jesus's righteousness—trusting in him, hiding in his righteousness, resting in the love he brings us from the Father— we will step out in confidence.

This is just what the apostle Paul means when he talks about "the righteousness of God through faith in Jesus Christ for all who believe" (Rom. 3:22). God declares all believers in Jesus to be spotlessly righteous. Paul learned to turn his back on his own efforts to be good, saying, "I consider them garbage, that I may gain Christ and be found in him, not having a righteousness of my own that comes from the law, but that which is through faith in Christ—the righteousness that comes from God on the basis of faith" (Phil. 3:8–9 NIV). This is the pattern of authentic Christian faith. It's not what I (Lewis) have done, but what Christ has done for me.

In a sermon published in 1519, Martin Luther declared that "through faith in Christ, Christ's righteousness becomes our righteousness and all that he has becomes ours; rather, he himself becomes ours."[19] Jesus comes to us and gives us all of his perfect righteousness. We receive this through faith. Everything else, says Paul, is rubbish in contrast to this amazing gift!

So we wear Jesus's righteousness. He is all we need to stand secure before God, defiant against Satan, and confident before the world. Discipleship is not about appeasing an angry God, or retreating from a difficult world. Discipleship is wearing the breastplate of righteousness, knowing that in Christ, God loves you unconditionally and that in the strength of his love you can stand in all trials.

## Reflect

1. Can you identify any of the wrong armor you instinctively put on when you feel afraid? What is it? What does God's unconditional love in Jesus for you say to that instinct?

2. Pray for a deeper faith to believe that in Jesus you really are declared righteousness and have nothing to fear. Only the Spirit can work that conviction in you. So why not ask him to do it?

## Pray

*Lord, I spend so much of my life trying to feel safe. People can scare me, situations overwhelm me, and I even scare myself sometimes. My efforts don't work. I rest again in your love, Lord Jesus. Thank you that all of your life you were so brave as you always trusted your Father. Thank you that you died heaped with my sin so that I might be clothed in your perfection. I stand and I worship dressed in your righteousness. Hallelujah! Amen.*

PART 6

---

# GOD'S WORD: PRIZING THE POWER

Amy knows that the Bible is special. She listens to it preached every Sunday, and often she's deeply stirred. She comes to Bible studies fairly regularly, and there are times when she's really struck by what she learns. Sometimes, Amy opens up her Bible on her own. Her work friends have her down as "super-religious," but Amy wishes she knew and really loved her Savior more and felt more confident about his love for her. She knows she's missing out, and she knows that the way to know God is to go deeper in his word. It's just that she's not sure how to, and isn't confident that anything could ever be any different.

All Christians need God's word. This part is an invitation to reflect on God's gift of his word, the Bible. Through his word, God reveals himself to us as the Lord of undeniable authority, and of tender covenant faithfulness. He also promises us that his Spirit can create a hunger in us to hear and to respond to his truth in life-changing ways. And the same Spirit can work a deep confidence in us that the Bible really is true in a world where there are so many lies, and keep us in that certainty even when life is really tough.

What Amy needs (and what we all need) is specific guidance in how to get into God's word and to build good routines and habits. Before those are in place (and we'll come to them in turn), we need the strongest conviction that the Bible is the treasure it claims to be. We'll be exploring two images the apostle Paul gives us in Ephesians 6:14, 16—the belt of truth and the sword of the Spirit. If the Bible is not special, we will make no special efforts with it. So we'll be checking our hearts, making sure that we appreciate just how unique Scripture is, as the sword of the Spirit, and just how massive a privilege we face as we come to it.

Then we'll look at the struggles we all experience to enjoy God's word consistently, and see how we can take heart in God's power to give us an appetite for his truth. That will then lead us to reflect on how we must prize the belt of truth, the Bible.

14

# The Sharp Edge

Do You Know the Power of God's Word?

*Take . . . the sword of the Spirit, which is the word of God.*
EPHESIANS 6:17

AS PAUL LISTS the soldier's protective armor in Ephesians 6, he includes just one weapon, the sword. For the believer, this is "the sword of the Spirit, the Word of God" (Eph. 6:17). The word of God means all of the inspired words God has breathed out and caused to be recorded in the pages of Scripture. This means the gospel of God, his astonishing and life-changing good news message of sins forgiven through faith in Jesus Christ. Alongside that gospel message, his word comes with all of God's promises, his warnings, his commandments, and his encouragements. God's word is rich and full. But we will only experience that when we take hold of it.

If we are to have an authentic experience of God through his word, we must take hold of our Bibles with fresh conviction about its power and hunger to experience that power. Do you remember the great reality of your conversion to Christ as you believed the message of the Bible? "You accepted it not as the word of men but as what it really is, the word of God, which is at work in you believers" (1 Thess. 2:13). That is true of every Christian. God brought you from death to life, from darkness to life, and from hell to heaven. Now he wants to continue that transformation, as his Spirit brings that word into your heart, so that you experience life, light, and a foretaste of heaven, all in a rich knowledge of his love for you in Christ. Only the word brings that to you. Take hold of it!

His word is so powerful. As the Bible teacher John Stott put it, "Still today it is his sword, for he still uses it to cut through people's defenses, to prick their consciences, and to stab them spiritually awake. Yet he also puts his sword into our hands, so that we may use it both in resisting temptation (as Jesus did, quoting Scripture to counter the devil in the Judean wilderness) and in evangelism."[20] The sword is sharp, and no less sharp today than it was when God first gave it. How could it be? It is his dynamic, speaking voice.

## No Power except His

There are so many promises of power in the Christian world today. Our friend David was eager to know how he could fight back against the sins that seemed to hold him fast. He needed power, but his life became an exhausting chase for the right experience. Maybe if he went to this meeting, worshiped in that way, said those words, or took on this prayer technique, then he would encounter God and his troubles would disappear. Heaven knows, he tried. Nothing worked, though. Nothing worked. The devil and his discouragements were all too apparent in his life. He felt wretched and became dangerously cynical about his faith. Despite the talk he heard, there was no power to help him.

Looking back on that period many months later, David realized that, for all of his activities and effort, the word of God hardly had any place in them. He hadn't put his Bible away and forgotten it; but he had effectively forgotten it since he wasn't reading it expecting that the word would address his struggles and bring him powerful solutions. As David learned to wrestle again with what the Bible had to say about his problems, and to bring those lessons into the details of his life, hope as well as real progress returned. It wasn't overnight (lasting change rarely is) but today he is treasuring God's word in new ways, and it's bearing fruit in his life. He is learning to bring the sword of the Spirit to his problems. That is true discipleship.

We must allow this sharp sword to do its work. In the military world, the Gurkha regiments, who serve with British and other armies, are famous for their bravery and skill in fighting. Their knife, the *khukuri*, is a fearsome weapon. The tradition goes that the Gurkha must never unsheathe his khukuri unless he draws blood with it. In other words, he must only use it when it's absolutely essential, and then, he must always use it for its sole purpose, to kill his enemy.

Not thoughts for the squeamish, perhaps! And yet, we must remember why God has given us his word. He wants us to stand firm in the victory Christ has won for us, to live as "more than conquerors through him who loved us" (Rom. 8:37). If we're going to fight sin and Satan, we must take a decisive hold of God's truth. Waving the Bible under our eyes for a few minutes here and there simply won't bring change. The word must enter us and possess us. We must make sure that its truth penetrates deeply, even when that's uncomfortable. "For the word of God is living and active, sharper than any two-edged sword, piercing to the division of soul and of spirit, of joints and of marrow, and discerning the thoughts and intentions of the heart. And no creature is hidden from his sight, but all are naked and exposed to the eyes of him to whom we must give account" (Heb. 4:12–13).

## Under the Sword

Naked and exposed? Pierced, even? Who wants that for themselves? Our sinful natures don't, but the Spirit wants to make us like the man of the word, Jesus Christ. Sin makes us hide from God, but God's word leads us out of our natural selves and deeper into the life of Christ. He submitted to God's word, even when that meant his becoming actually naked, exposed and pierced at the cross. His discipleship was radical and flawless. He was set free from selfishness and fear so that he could conquer for us through his obedience. His pattern—costly, but totally liberated—is ours too (see 1 Pet. 2:21).

So we commit ourselves to growing to be more like Jesus. This is why we need to wield the sword of the Spirit. We need to access the promises, commands, and encouragements of God for every thought, feeling, and situation, just as Jesus did. As we do that, we discover their power to change how we think and feel about the places we find ourselves in. The Scripture ministered by the Holy Spirit renews our minds and retrains our desires, and we become like our Master. That is our greatest calling and privilege. We get to trade in our old life, desperately seeking meaning and pleasure in the passing things of the world, and take up the life of Christ, finding him in his word and being shaped by his Spirit.

For you have been born again, not of perishable seed, but of imperishable, through the living and enduring word of God. For,

"All people are like grass,
and all their glory is like the flowers of the field;
the grass withers and the flowers fall,
but the word of the Lord endures forever."

And this is the word that was preached to you. (1 Pet. 1:24–25 NIV)

### Reflect

1. Are you confident that you will encounter God through his word? Why or why not?

2. How have you discovered that God's word is "sharp"? Think of a time when the word has got under all of your defenses and brought change in your life. What has that change been?

3. Write out some verses from the Bible that speak of the Bible's power and authority. (You might choose from statements in

Psalms 19 and 119.) Commit a couple of them to memory to encourage yourself about God's word.

## Pray

*Lord, thank you for your word! Thank you that you've promised to share your life with me as I meet you in the Bible. I don't have the wisdom or the power to live for Jesus, but you've given me all that I need in your word. Forgive me when I take up your word half-heartedly and sometimes just ignore it. Please give me a new thirst to engage with what you're saying to me, and may I hear the voice of the good shepherd guiding me each step of the way. Amen.*

15

# Confession Time

## Bring Your Heart to the God Who Cares

*Create in me a clean heart, O God,*
*and renew a right spirit within me.*

PSALM 51:10

HERE'S THE THING: our appetite for the Bible is often hit-and-miss. Sometimes we can't put it down, at other times, we can't pick it up. We know we should get into the word, we know that it's good for us, we've experienced its life-giving power, and we even want to go deeply into it. Our hearts leap when we hear the Psalmist say,

> Oh how I love your law!
>     It is my meditation all the day. (Ps. 119:97)

We know what he means. The Bible has a way of winning our hearts, and its power to guide and comfort amazes us. And then, our love for the word just seems to fade away. The word we loved is the word we now want to avoid. Why?

The reasons for this can be many. People can say that the Bible's "boring" or "not relevant," and we might wonder if they've got a point. Actually, we know that our problem with Bible reading is that it's *too* relevant. Its instructions and warnings and reminders are far sharper than we are often comfortable with. It's not that the Bible doesn't speak into our lives; sometimes it just speaks far too loudly. If we're honest, we often prefer to stay in our own private world, cocooned in our own values and agendas, even when that means having a weak, doubting faith, or a sin that robs us of joy. Sometimes experiencing the invasion of God's truth, bringing light into our darkest places, is just too much.

We must be confident that where Jesus is through his word, he brings light and life. Yes, he will say painful things to us at times. When he speaks the truth, though, he always speaks it in love. It comes back to what we were thinking about change. If we don't want change, we can hold Jesus at arm's length. If, on the other hand, we're hungry to change, and eager to stand firm, then we need to ask the Holy Spirit to develop an appetite in us for his life-giving word. And he will.

Truth is always hard for us to bear. The poet T. S. Eliot said, "Humankind cannot bear very much reality."[21] His contemporary C. S. Lewis famously likened us to children contenting themselves with playing in the mud because they refused to believe there could be anything as glorious as the sea.[22] They're both right, as we know. The greatest reality, the most glorious ocean, is the gospel, which the Spirit longs to work more and more deeply in our hearts. We are loved, deeply and unconditionally. God the Father has willed and planned our salvation, God the Son has achieved it through his spotless life, perfect death, triumphant resurrection, and ascension into heaven. The Spirit has come from the Father and the Son to bring conviction of our sin, of God's perfect law, and of the judgment we deserve deep into our proud hearts, and then he has shown us that all of our wrong-doing was taken by our substitute, Jesus. We have full forgiveness and life in him. We simply cannot be more loved.

## Truth Loves, Lies Hate

When someone is talking to you who you know really loves you and has your wellbeing front and center, you can trust what he or she says, even if it sometimes hurts. Putting the belt of truth on means learning to trust God more and more through being willing to listen to him. Remember, all that he tells us is for our good, so that we might be more joyful followers of Jesus, whatever is happening in our lives. Then we will truly be standing firm.

Believe God's truth or Satan's lies? Whom we choose to listen to determines whom we end up believing. God has said that we can be absolutely certain of his love in Jesus. Knowing that certainty deep within has the power to change us from doubt to confident faith. Small wonder, then, that Satan will do all he can to keep us from listening to our Lord. Listen to the Puritan Pastor Thomas Brooks:

> Such is Satan's envy and enmity against a Christian's joy and comfort that he cannot but act to the utmost of his line to keep poor souls in doubt and darkness. Satan knows that assurance

is a pearl of that price that will make the soul happy forever: he knows that assurance makes a Christian's wilderness to be a paradise; he knows that assurance begets in Christians the most noble and generous spirits; He knows that assurance is that which will make men strong to do exploits, to shake his tottering kingdom about his ears; and therefore he is very studious and industrious to keep souls out of assurance as he was to cast Adam out of paradise.[23]

What's Brooks saying? He's saying that the devil hates our confidence in Jesus. He hates it because he knows that it brings us joy and has a power to transform doubting, hesitant faith into bold, decisive action for our Savior. He will do anything he can to undermine our faith in Christ, and those lies and accusations we've already seen are central to his plan. Listen to them, though, and you've lost. Listen to the promises of God's grace and you will stand victoriously in Jesus. He is the truth who defeats Satan. Believe him as you listen to him.

### Ask Him to Build Your Appetite

If you're going to listen to his truth, you must first have the appetite to do so. And as people still afflicted by sin, we shouldn't be surprised that our hunger for God's word is so variable. When one of our sons was six, he had a collapsed lung, pneumonia, and additional complications, and he was in the hospital for eleven days. He was fed by a drip for over a week. He couldn't eat solid food, and he didn't want to. I (Lewis) can remember fighting back tears of joy and relief when I fed him his first mouthfuls of cereal. I had no doubt at that point that he would recover. Just so, our heavenly Father knows that sin robs us of our appetite for his word; and yet, he has the power to renew that desire in us and longs to do so.

So we struggling saints must pray. Think about the prayer of David, crushed by his sins of adultery, lies, and murder. He begs of the Lord,

> Create in me a clean heart, O God,
>     and renew a right spirit within me. (Ps. 51:10)

He knows that he cannot trust his heart. He must entrust it to another. We need to do the same. Our lives might not have imploded as David's did, but we can and must ask him to purify us deep within. That's when we will see his Spirit creating new desires for him and his word.

We can pray no better prayer than the one David prays in Psalm 86, when he asks,

> Teach me your way, O LORD,
>     that I may walk in your truth;
>     unite my heart to fear your name. (Ps. 86.11)

Sin is the great heart-divider, taking us from our calling to love the Lord with our whole heart, soul, mind, and strength (Mark 12:30). Christians with divided hearts are miserable, unable to find true joy in either sin or in grace. What we need is the Spirit to give us a single heart, cleansed of warring desires, wholly focused on the Lord who wants to meet us in the pages of Scripture. And he will.

## Reflect

1. When are the times you love to read God's word? What factors can you see in your life that make you want to avoid it?

2. "Man shall not live by bread alone, / but by every word that comes from the mouth of God" (Matt. 4:4). How does this verse challenge you, and what might you do in response?

3. Have you ever brought your spiritual appetites to the Lord? Why or why not?

## Pray

*Lord, you have my heart, but please call my heart to a deeper, more joyful surrender to you. Where I am hiding from you, or reluctant to go deeper into your love, meet me and change me, Lord. Make me like your Son, who chose your word over even the best things of life, and set me on the narrow road of trusting obedience. I believe that in losing myself for him I will know his love, which is better than life. Amen.*

16

# Truth Wins

## Prizing the Bible

*Like newborn infants, long for the pure spiritual milk*
*. . . if indeed you have tasted that the Lord is good.*

I PETER 2:2–3

THE APOSTLE PAUL wants Christians to stand. In Ephesians 6:10–14, he says that we must stand a number of times.[24] Remember, Paul isn't speaking as someone who doesn't get how tough the Christian life is. There was no apostolic exemption from the trials of the discipleship. Paul knows full well that Christians may have to deal with stress, danger, financial hardship, illness, depression, accidents, loneliness, and persecution. Life has a way of beating up all of us. Sometimes it knocks us right over. Paul's life is a catalog of suffering. Nor is Paul suffering because he's not taking the Christian life seriously; it's precisely because he *is*

137

living wholeheartedly for Christ that he suffers. By God's magnificent grace he stood firm, and he's calling on fellow-believers to do the same.

## Standing in the Truth

As we're finding out, standing means discovering that we don't have the strength in ourselves to keep going as Christians. We're also learning that God has all of the strength in Christ that we need to face life. We may sometimes flatter ourselves that we are "strong" Christians, and that we're standing firm. Paul warns us, lovingly but firmly: "Let anyone who thinks that he stands take heed lest he fall" (1 Cor. 10:12). The moment we think we can do it on our own we are in the greatest danger. We don't have the resources for discipleship in ourselves. The gospel does.

The gospel is never something that we're given simply to save us from God's wrath, wonderful though that would be. Yes, we have an eternity of certain salvation won for us in the living, dying, rising, ruling, and returning of Jesus. Hallelujah! The gospel is also God's power working deeply within us in the here and now, to deliver us from every instinct to want to live life in our own strength, apart from the Lord and his love. Its message bores down into all that we are, and goes deep into our recesses of pride and proud self-reliance. Paul learned this, as he lived the gospel life. Through so many hardships he found out that he simply could not stand in his own strength. He learned, as we need to, that God wants to make us strong, as we trust in him totally.

So how do we stand? The very first thing we're commanded to put on of the whole armor of God is the belt of truth (Eph. 6:14).

The soldier's belt was a critical part of his equipment. It was pulled tightly over his loose-fitting tunic to bring it close to his body to allow him to move in combat, and his sword was then hung on it. So the belt is the first thing he put on as he got ready for battle. The belt of God's gospel truth is the first thing we need to reach for, if we're to withstand the attacks of Satan, and stand.

## Listen Up!

We need God's truth because our greatest enemy wants to get the truth out of our lives. Satan is a liar and father of lies. "Did God really say . . . ?" (Gen. 3:1 NIV) are his first words in Scripture, and they echo in every temptation in our hearts. Satan lies, and our hearts are tempted to believe his untruth. His attacks on God's children are relentless, and they come through his moment-by-moment barrage of lies and accusations. He simply never ever tells the truth, but grinds us down as we succumb to his whispers. His is a subtle and slow work, often invisible, carried on in the depths of our minds and hearts. He whispers to us, and unsettles our confidence in Christ's love for us. He puts doubts about God's sovereign lordship over the apparent chaos of life and of our lives. More than anything, he loves to accuse us all over again about those sins we thought we had peace about through Christ's blood. What will deliver us from this monster? Only the truth of God. We can only fight him if we surround ourselves with God's truth.

We will never put on the belt of truth unless we're absolutely convinced about what it is and why we need it. The truth is the Son of God, and all that is given to us in him. Jesus is the great enemy and defeater of Satan, and while we are relying on him in all of his truth, we are safe against the devil's lies.

All of the Bible is ultimately a revelation of Jesus, pointing to the hope and destiny of the world as being found in him. God-breathed, free from any error, the living and powerful declaration of God himself: these are just some of the ways the Bible speaks of itself. All of those claims are true of every book, page, line, and word of the Bible. Each is the work of the Spirit of God their author, and in all he is unfailingly pointing us to Jesus. This gorgeous, glorious, true, and living word has been placed into our hands. Will we take it?

We have a choice. When Satan's lies and discouragements threaten to overwhelm us, will we embrace God's truth or avoid it? Will we give it a quick glance, or will we give it our attention, not because we think we should, but because we know we need the promises and direction of the word?

God uses the Bible to accomplish the work of transformation in and then through us. Think of Paul's well-known declaration to Timothy: "All Scripture is breathed out by God and profitable for teaching, for reproof, for correction, and for training in righteousness, that the man of God may be complete, equipped for every good work" (2 Tim. 3:16–17). Do you see the purpose of God's word? It is given to produce *change*. As we are exposed to it, we are shaped and refined by it. Change is *inevitable*. That is both hard news (change is incredibly painful) and it is exciting and glorious news (God is not allowing us to stay in the darkness of destructive thoughts and behavior). He wants to bring glorious change. He wants to equip us to live on earth as the Lord Jesus himself did, complete and equipped for every good work. That is a thrilling prospect! Put the belt of truth on, and that is what is promised to you.

## Oh So Weak

Once Paul was tempted to feel proud because of all God had revealed to him. He tells the Corinthians that he was lashed by powerful temptations, the work of Satan himself. Well, we've had no apostolic visions, but we can surely relate to that. Prayer didn't take away Paul's agony, but God reassured him: "My grace is sufficient for you, for my power is made perfect in weakness" (2 Cor. 12:9). So what happened?

It's easier to say what didn't happen—the thorn in the flesh Paul experienced wasn't removed from his life. Where he was weak and tempted, he experienced the Holy Spirit ministering exactly the grace he needed. As that happened, a man so trained to rely on himself discovered new depths of real strength, God's sufficient grace. His outlook changed, he was humbled in worship, and God got the glory as Paul and those he served knew this strength was of the Lord: "Therefore I will boast all the more gladly of my weaknesses, so that the power of Christ may rest upon me. For the sake of Christ, then, I am content with weaknesses, insults, hardships, persecutions, and calamities. For when I am weak, then I am strong" (2 Cor. 12:9–10).

Could we ever be content with discovering just how powerless and weak we are? It sounds like a paradox, doesn't it? We spend our lives running from our weaknesses, even hiding from them, and often trying desperately to fix them. Parents, fellow students, work colleagues, the people we follow on social media, even our friends, all have the same message—*be the very best you can be.* The Bible does not disagree—God wants us to be the best we can be. But what is our best? God saves people in order to make them discover true greatness, as his passionate and joyful servants, trusting in him utterly, even when life is brutal. Our best is standing firm in faith, just like the Lord Jesus Christ, trusting God and offering our lives in his service.

The world may find that a strange definition of "best"; Christians are discovering, as Paul did, that there is no other life to live. God brings weakness into our lives and then uses it to bring out his very best for us: brave, persevering, moment-by-moment trust in him and fruitful living for his sake. The rest of our lives—study, work, relationships, and leisure interests—are the details in which we work it all out.

### Reflect

1. What is troubling you most in your life right now? Have you brought that pain to the Lord yet? If so, can you see his hand in your life, giving you help?

2. Consider Paul's statement in 2 Cor. 12:9, "I will boast all the more gladly of my weaknesses, so that the power of Christ may rest upon me." Do you want to experience the power of Christ, even in your weakest points? And now reflect on the following verse, "When I am weak, then I am strong" (v. 10).

3. Could you ever get to a place of acceptance of God's plan in your pain, this side of heaven? If so, do you think that would be a defeat or a victory?

## Pray

*Lord Jesus, you were content to be weak and vulnerable as you lived among us. You were also the bravest man who ever lived. Your strength was in your obedience to your Father's will and your utter trust in him.*

*Lord, please help me to take the brave steps of saying no to trusting in what I think I can do, and to relying on what you alone can do in my life. Lord, where I am weak, may I know you to be my strength. Amen.*

PART 7

———————

# GOD'S WORD:
# HEARTS AND HABITS

The Bible is a practical book, given to us to change the way we think, feel, and live. It is not a tome of theory, nor it is a collection of wise sayings for us to pick and choose from. At the close of his life, Moses said to the Israelites about his ministry of teaching God's word, "It is no empty word for you, but your very life" (Deut. 32:47). May God give us grace to recognize and take hold of the life he shares with us through his word. This is the book where we discover life in Christ. And for that life to flow into us and work its transforming power, we must discover how to get the word into us, each day, and for every situation. This is what this part is about.

First of all, we'll be looking at the power of habits, good and bad, and thinking about how to form really helpful habits in reading our Bibles. As a pastor, I (Lewis) spend time almost every week encouraging members of our church family to get into the Bible and to get a nourishing daily diet of God's word. Some are newer to the faith or new to our church with its high view of Scripture, and it's a struggle for them. Others struggle because it's a good habit they've fallen out of and find it hard to relearn. Wherever we're from, all Christians need to learn how to get into the word. Without good habits, Bible reading is never more than hit or miss, and usually just becomes miss, unless we're very careful. We need to address that. Next, there's the challenge of reading the Bible well, really allowing it to get to work in us, penetrating our natural defenses so that its life-changing power takes effect by the Spirit. It's when we take the time to slow down with God's word and open our hearts up to it unhurriedly that we know in a thrilling way that the Lord wants to teach and transform us.

As we grow to love Scripture, we will feel our privileged responsibility of taking what we're learning to others. The final chapter of this part helps us to think about how we speak to others for their encouragement in Christ. If God is speaking to us in his word, we are privileged to share words of grace with a needy world.

17

# Hold On!

## Creating and Keeping Healthy Bible Habits

*. . . the word of his grace, which is able to build you up.*

ACTS 20:32

NO ONE SEES JEZ'S BATTLES. Depression keeps him stuck at home much of the time. Jez isn't working at the moment, and the days (and nights) can pass incredibly slowly. His life is far harder than most people's I know, but spending time with him is a real privilege as I (Lewis) always come away humbled by and deeply grateful for the grace of God at work. Jez has learned to see the world and his life not through the lens of his problems, but from the perspective of the word of God. He is committed to loving his Bible and his Savior. Life is so hard, but Jez's hardships aren't the final word—God's promises of grace, help, and hope are. And that makes every possible difference for him and for all of us.

If we're to stand in the battle, we must really know God's gospel truth for ourselves in the deepest places of our hearts. We must be convinced that God's word is true, truer even than what our circumstances and our hearts' longings are telling us. Think of Isaiah's warning to the king of his day:

If you do not stand firm in your faith,
   you will not stand at all. (Isa. 7:9 NIV)

In other words, when there's crisis, danger, or threat, then that's the time to be sure that God can be utterly relied upon, because his truth has already won our trust. We need to have the truth of the word so deeply in us that we are deeply convinced that it is true.

This means, quite obviously, that if we're to stand firm, we need to be committed to engaging with God's word. We need to develop habits that bless us so that we get the word of Christ dwelling in us richly. We can only walk with Jesus if we're listening to his guiding voice (John 10:3–4). Those listening habits need to be put into place, which impact us weekly, daily, and moment by moment.

Before we explore helpful ways to get into the Bible, let's think about habits. Good habits are usually really hard to pick up—our lives are already so full of bad ones! Many people think that dieting or exercise or early mornings aren't that hard, until they try them. Picking up bad habits takes no effort at all, and usually we don't realize we're doing them: negative moods, proud words, or carefully hidden and sinful use of money, internet, and phone. We obsess about things, habitually and destructively. Even what feels like impulse behavior—splurging money on purchases we don't really need, wrong ways of using food or alcohol—are often habits we've slowly given into over time rather than sudden urges that came out of nowhere. And yet, growth in loving Jesus more and becoming like him comes down to the power of Spirit-shaped habits of living well. Yes, good habits are incredibly hard to form. Disciplined habits with eating, exercise, screen-time, all take effort and intention. But they're far from impossible by God's grace, and the joy and freedom they bring are incredible. Reading God's word is a habit, and its effects bring more joy and freedom than anything else we could do. It takes time to form this habit into our lives, but the Holy Spirit is the power of God to make this habit stick for our great good.

So if your Bible reading has been a disaster, or at least far from what you want, don't despair: the Spirit who gave the word longs to bring the word to us. We need to find the ways we can open ourselves to that word, and do so again and again, until tentative steps become the habit we acquire, maybe without even realizing it. He will help us with just that. Here are five simple steps to great Bible reading:

*1. Fight for Time.* Make time, stick to time, and guard time. We need to start a commitment to God's word by giving it time. If regular Bible reading is new to you, it will help you greatly if you decide to commit to the same time (pretty much) every day, finding a quiet place and time slot where you're alert and not too distracted. Everyone's different, but it's hard to beat making Bible reading the very first thing you do each day. As the day goes on, your mind gets more crowded, time is more pressured, and it's a bigger battle to stop and give attention to God's word. And besides, if we want God to go with us into the day, shouldn't we be hearing from him first thing?

*2. Have a Plan.* Don't read whatever you feel like in Scripture— a verse here, a chapter there—but instead find a good method of systematic reading. Go through books of the Bible, with a helpful book or podcast to help you learn, if you can. Aim to hear something from both the Old and the New Testament each day. Experiment with ways of reading the Bible and different amounts you can cover. Get advice and compare your habits with those of your friends.

*3. Get Help.* Unless you're careful, Bible reading can be all too mechanical and passive. Find ways to be an active reader, helping yourself to benefit from your Bible. Reading out loud is a great way to keep concentrating, so that God's word really engages you. Write down your thoughts, either in your Bible itself, in a notebook, or on your phone. Underline what strikes you, even write out key verses. Put those verses on your phone, and set them as reminders to bring your mind back to God's word through the day. Get recommendations for Bible notes or devotionals, and experiment with them. Challenge yourself to memorize passages that minister to you. That is really the best way to know Scripture truth.

*4. Be Accountable.* Talk and discuss. Is there a friend you can swap texts with, sharing one verse or lesson that's struck you from your reading? Sharing Scripture is a great way of being kept sharp, and it helps us to read the Bible more attentively, knowing that we'll be talking about it with others.

*5. Remember the Purpose.* Bible reading is not an end in itself. Bible reading is about looking beyond life's trials and embracing God's love in Christ as we fix our hearts on his promises. Enjoy that love, and discover how solid a rock it is when life is tough. You'll discover practical guidance and overarching reassurance for each problem and challenge. My friend Jez can stand, despite everything, because he is a man of the word. And so can you.

As people of the Spirit-ministered word, the apostle Paul says,

> We do not lose heart. Though our outer self is wasting away, our inner self is being renewed day by day. For this light momentary affliction is preparing for us an eternal weight of glory beyond all comparison, as we look not to the things that are seen but to the things that are unseen. For the things that are seen are transient, but the things that are unseen are eternal. (2 Cor. 4:16–18)

## Reflect

1. J. I. Packer writes that "habit forming is the Spirit's ordinary way of leading us on in holiness."[25] Are you open to putting off some habits and putting on the practice of engaging with God's word meaningfully each day as God helps you? Be honest and be specific.

2. What pattern of regular Bible reading will you choose? Think about the amount of Bible you'll engage with, what time or times

in the day, and whether you will use any notes or phone apps to help your reading. Make a note of your decisions below.

3. Is there a person or a small group you could get support from as you get into disciplined Bible reading? When will you approach them about this?

**Pray**

*Lord, I'm such a mix of different desires and longings! Forgive me that my appetite for you is often so weak. Give me grace to pursue you in your word in both the joys and the pains of life. Please give me a hunger for your word and meet me and deepen my love for you as you reveal yourself to me. Shape me to be like your dear Son, who always trusted you and stood firm on your word. For his sake, amen.*

18

# Take It to Heart

## God's Word for Our Deep Needs

*I have stored up your word in my heart,*
*that I might not sin against you.*

PSALM 119:11

A FRIEND OF MINE who was in the Royal Navy told me that submariners call those who serve on surface boats "skimmers." Of course, we're meant to hear the insinuation that underwater is where the real action is. Submariners relish the silent world of the depths and seem to enjoy the mystery surrounding what they do.

## Skimmers or Deep-Divers?

Are you a skimmer when it comes to God's word? Skimming the pages of Scripture, reading in order to have "done your daily reading" will not develop our faith. Growing Christians are those who are learning how to go deeper into the word. It is as we learn to think slowly and carefully about the truth of Scripture that we will discover its power to transform us in lasting ways.

It's not enough to talk about the Bible, if it's not actually speaking to us. Nor will it make any difference if we say we love the Bible, but are effectively just distant friends. God has called us to be people of his word, who are going deeper into our relationships with him as we seek out what he has to say and learn to trust him. We must obey his call.

### Can't Even . . .

First, let's be honest about how distracted we get. We want to read our Bibles, but something crops up. We start our reading, only to be interrupted and not get back to it. And if you read your Bible on your phone, you have a literal world of distraction at your fingertips. Our faith is small and the world is a big, busy place that is always demanding our attention. The bigger truth is that the devil's in the distraction, and we need to recognize that, and work out how he's distracting us from God's word. Then we need to do something about it.

To understand his strategies, start to think like Satan. If you were the devil, with a mission to tempt believers like you, what would you go for? You could use the X-rated sins and get them to topple into the more graphic sins of sex, money, and alcohol abuse. That would take a few down and has worked well. Most Christians are a more cautious bunch, though, and finding their way (even without your diabolical help) toward those sins might be more than they would do. How about a more effective and more subtle strategy? Surely you would keep them from God's word? How simple and how effective. A word-less Christian is like someone who doesn't eat. They become light-headed and eventually fall over. That's all you would need to do. And it would be deadly.

So as you go on your imagined devilish business, just nudge them about deep-seated guilt over sins and get them fixated on their all-round badness. Or give them enough distraction in the busyness (or boredom) of everyday life. That should do it. Anything to keep them from their Bibles. Because, as we all know, no word, no growth. And no sword of the Spirit. We'd only be able to stand when he attacks, but not get on the offensive ourselves to wound him.

Well, that's the devil at work. If we're to be resilient Christians, we must get to work too and counter his schemes. We've already looked at how to develop a regular Bible diet (in chapter 17). Let's think now about how we add unhurried times that allow for going deeper into that word and bringing it very specifically to life's challenges.

As we open our Bibles we're not hunting for hidden knowledge or undiscovered keys to spiritual power. We are recognizing, on the other hand, that growing more like Jesus as we battle sin means having such a grasp of spiritual truth that it goes deeply into our hearts and minds. "Do not be conformed to this world, but be transformed by the renewal of your mind" (Rom. 12:2). "I have stored up your word in my heart, / that I might not sin against you" (Ps. 119:11). These verses encourage us that as we take hold of the word, we will discover that that word takes hold of us. The German Reformer Martin Luther allegedly said, "The words of our Savior Christ are exceedingly powerful; they have hands and feet."[26] Jesus comes to us in his word. He takes hold of us in loving authority. We yield to his lordship and grace. And we submit to his will in our lives, confident that he will meet us by his Spirit to help us fight sin. But only if we're serious with his word.

## Focus!

Daily reading is essential. We need to add to daily reading intentional times of unhurried reflection and meditation on God's word. Liam found himself one summer as a new believer leading at two Christian youth camps, back to back. The first youth camp experience was incredibly intense, and in his youthful zeal Liam took on far too much than was wise. A couple of days into the second youth camp, he discovered he was absolutely spent. He didn't like the camp or the activities, and to his embarrassment he realized that he had little love for the kids he was called to serve. He was in trouble. So one afternoon Liam traded his duties and slipped outside for a break. He turned to the passage on love in 1 Corinthians 13:1–8. For almost two hours Liam walked through the countryside with that passage in his hands. He read it out loud slowly, phrase by phrase, again and again. He lingered over each word. Sometimes the words were so powerful, and Liam was so moved by them, that he just stood still, letting their truths break over and envelop him as God's grace ministered to him. He prayed those words into his life again. It was a powerful encounter with the Lord Jesus, the Lord of patient, self-giving love. Liam's vision was cleared, and his heart deeply refreshed. He was ready again to serve in the Lord's strength.

I (Lewis) am sure you have testimonies of the Lord's way of refreshing you like this. I hope you do. Certainly, we all need to pursue him in intentional, unhurried ways. So alongside your daily Bible times, plan to invest in longer times with the Lord.

Also, learn the power of God's word memorized. That is a way like no other to have it stored up in your heart (Ps. 119:11). The remembered word is the sharpest weapon immediately to hand in the fight against sin. When temptation comes, God's Spirit takes the word that we have put in our hearts and wields it with us. We discover that the verses we've trained ourselves to remember have been at work deep below the surface, changing our attitudes and our loves.

Our town of Huddersfield is close to beautiful moorland scenery, with big skies and a summer covering of purple heather. Every summer, though, the moors are in danger of fire. Dry spells are deadly, and, with just a stray spark, flames can devastate for many miles around. So it is with the soul. Without God's quenching word, even the smallest temptation can start a deadly fire of sin. We don't know when that temptation will come, but if we're soaked in the truths of Scripture, it's going to be a lot harder for temptation to start its fire in us.

Think about the fight against pride: "I mustn't be proud, I must be humble" is a good thing to tell ourselves, but those commands alone won't help us make much progress. We need to hear the Bible's warnings against pride. We need to dwell on the verses that tell us how much human pride is an affront to God's glory and is so destructive to our souls. We then need to see the beauty and freedom of pride's opposite—humility—as Jesus embodies it. A quick online Bible search will give us a handful of key verses on both pride's evil and humility's goodness. If pride is a key battleground, we should select the few verses we need most, write them out, and commit them to memory.

As we do so, the Spirit stores them in our hearts and uses them in our affections. He gives us a new repulsion at pride's ugliness and a new hunger for the beauty of a humble life seen in Christ, as we follow our Master. The Spirit-led life means commitment and effort on our part. But be encouraged: the Spirit is for us and fighting with us. We are never, ever alone!

As the psalmist says, "I will run in the way of your commandments / when you enlarge my heart!" (119:32). Bible-saturated and Spirit-led hearts know this joy. May God give us grace to pursue him and to run with perseverance and joy the way marked out for us in Christ Jesus.

### Reflect

1. What are your particular struggles at the moment? Have you discovered yet what God's word says for your encouragement and guidance about them?

2. Collect some key verses to memorize to help you in your discipleship in these areas and jot them below.

3. Memorizing Scripture can feel like a big step if you're new to it. Is there someone you can share the challenge with?

4. Spend some time thanking the Lord that because of Jesus he is totally for you and has the love and power to help you in your struggles.

## Pray

*Lord Jesus, you are my conqueror and my captain. Thank you that you broke the reign of sin in my life when you died and rose, and that you will give me all that I need as you lead me to heaven. Help me not to be afraid of the battle because you are with me and give me deep confidence in your word as I feed upon it. For your sake, amen.*

19

# Sharing the Word

## Learning to Minister Jesus in How We Speak

*Encourage one another and build one another up.*

1 THESSALONIANS 5:11

HILARY HAD THE BIGGEST SMILE in the room whenever our group got together. She was always positive and always really sensitive toward others. Hilary just had the knack of bringing the right words to a person. No surprise that others often sought her out when they were having a tough time. Sometimes, though, even if for just a moment, Hilary would look away and her smile would fade. This happy young lady had her sorrows too and desperately needed encouragement. It took us a long time to realize that and to recognize that we had failed her by assuming that she was always okay. I (Lewis) hope we learned that everyone needs the ministry of encouraging words.

One of the ways we take up the sword of the Spirit against the devil is to speak encouragement to one another. When a fellow Christian is struggling, he or she needs to hear reassuring gospel words from another believer. The devil attacks us all, and we need to look out for and help each other as we face his attacks. Paul has already told the Christians at Ephesus that one key priority as we grow into maturity is that we "speak the truth in love" (Eph. 4:15 NLT). This is a core way we serve others in the body of Christ, bringing the reminders, promises, warnings, and many encouragements of the Bible to each other. It's also a crucial part of our growing in grace as Christians. In this chapter, we're thinking about how we can speak encouragement more effectively.

## Just Words? Never!

Don't underestimate the massive power your words have to breathe encouragement into fellow struggling disciples. We all know the power of words, either to devastate or to strengthen us. The Bible recognizes that words can bring blessing or misery. Reflect on Proverbs 12:18: "There is one whose rash words are like sword thrusts, / but the tongue of the wise brings healing." We've all experienced the sharp pain of things said to us that have gone deep. Sometimes they have been true, and the pride or some other sin we've been nursing has taken a heavy blow. Not always, though. Careless and loveless words wound when we are unfairly criticized. There are times we've needed a gentle encouragement but have received a lecture, instead. Sometimes, our hearts have been crying out for someone to say anything to lift our spirits, but no one has spoken. As we approach one another in the body of Christ, we need to be relying on God's Spirit that we might have just the right words to say, and be empowered to say them in the right way. We need to grow in how we use our words, so (as another Proverbs verse says) others discover that "gracious words are like a honeycomb, / sweetness to the soul and health to the body" (16:24).

"Gracious words" bring the reality of God's grace in Christ to people in need of just that. They're not a pat on the back, they're not empty compliments, and they're certainly not insincere words meant to make a person feel good when his real needs are avoided. Jesus didn't flatter anyone. He spoke what people needed to hear, always. Listening to Jesus is our masterclass in learning how to speak truthful, grace-filled words. As others hear them, they learn that God can be trusted and that following Jesus brings the strength we need to navigate life's journey.

The picture in Hebrews 4:12–13 is of the word opening us up, right to the hidden places of who we are. In one sense, we shouldn't be surprised—this is God's word, after all. Nothing can blunt it, not even our sin or sinful unbelief. Maybe we do need that reminder, though. When our friends are going through tough times we so often feel powerless to help them and wonder if anything can help them. But something can help, and that is the word of God. We need to reach out to them in love, as we handle that word with great care, bringing the right Scripture to their deep heart needs.

The command to speak the truth in love shines helpful light on the apostle Peter's command that a Christian should speak "as one who speaks the oracles of God" (1 Pet. 4:11). He's not talking about the first-century gift of prophecy, giving infallible utterance as the Lord's spokesmen. What Peter is saying is that the word of God should be so in our hearts that it comes out on our lips as we minister it for the blessing of others. We see people struggling, and we long to bless them with the truth that is feeding and strengthening us for their sake. This is speaking the truth in love.

## You Can Do It—and You Must

A young adult in our congregation felt we needed an encouraging note, so she sent us one. In this case, it wasn't a text or an email but a card with an envelope and stamp—just like the old days we grew up in! She filled the card with well-chosen words and a verse of Scripture, and as we read it our hearts were filled with joy and strength. The Lord used this wonderful and dear friend to bless us. We read her words, and our eyes pricked with tears. We felt so privileged to have such a sister in Christ. For her it made no difference at all that we were her parents' age or that we had been following Jesus over thirty years, compared with her year in the Christian faith. She saw a couple in need of encouragement, and she brought it to us. We were thrilled and so grateful.

As we speak God's truth to one another with a transparent concern for others' well-being, we are quite simply doing God's work. That is a stunning thought. What an amazing privilege the Father has given us! Weak and doubting sinners are entrusted with the will of God, to carry out his holy purposes. Remember Hilary: she shared God's encouragement, and she needed to receive it too. That's the Christian life.

Never underestimate the good that you will discover encouraging words doing in your own heart. There is nothing like bringing God's word to a brother or sister in need to jolt us out of our introspection and the endless labyrinth of our struggles and feelings. It's as we share the powerful truths of God's grace with a friend that we hear them for what they are, truly life-giving. Gloriously, this stepping outside of what's preoccupying us as we give ourselves to someone else brings us, in time, back to our world again strengthened by the very word we've been sharing. Have you discovered this, yet? If not, then don't wait!

**Reflect**

1. Who in your life speaks words that really bless you? Thank God for them. What is it about how they speak that so encourages you?

2. Even people who weren't on Jesus's side had to admit, "No one ever spoke like this man!" (John 7:46). What strikes you about how Jesus spoke to people, and what makes him unique?

3. Taking up our crosses means putting to death the urges to promote ourselves, talk about what we want to, or talk over others. Have you noticed any ways you might be doing that? Maybe you could be brave enough to ask a trusted friend if they're hearing anything from you that is discouraging to others?

4. Who are some people the Lord has placed in your life for you to encourage? What sort of words do they need from you at the moment? Pray about this and commit to being a blessing to them.

## Pray

*Lord, I often make a mess of your gift of speech. I am so sorry and ask you to forgive me. Please help me be more aware of what others need from me when I open my mouth. Teach me to be slow to speak and quick to listen. Give me your Spirit's sensitivity when I do speak and help me to bring Christ's encouragement when I do so. For his name's sake, amen.*

# PART 8

# PRAYING

Prayer is God's gift to his people. We are called to enter our Father's presence in prayer, to lay our needs before him, confident in his love through his Son and of his help by his Holy Spirit. Exhausted and troubled souls often either forget to pray or simply refuse to. Life grinds them down and becomes an exhausting round of worries, responsibilities, and choices. As we study prayer, we'll discover that God wants us to share our deepest needs with him. There is much from the apostle's command that we pray (Eph. 6:18–19) for us to learn from.

We also bring others and their struggles to him in prayer. The experience of interceding for others has an amazing and transforming effect on us as the Spirit works. We discover a genuine love for those we pray for, and learn to be meaningfully invested in their good in Christ as we intercede for them.

So, as we build our trust in God and our appetite for prayer, this part closes with some specific pointers for how we can get praying, keep on praying, and know the thrill of trusting, love-fueled prayer. An exciting journey is ahead of all of us, to discover just how ready God is to pour his strengthening grace into our lives as we seek his face for all of our needs.

20

# Depend

Discover the Freedom of Relying on the Lord

*Praying at all times in the Spirit.*
EPHESIANS 6:18

NOT MANY OF US enjoy asking for things when we've got a problem. Asking for directions when we're lost, advice when we're confused, help when we're in a mess at work, or an honest conversation when we feel we've been let down by a friend: these things don't come easily to anyone. Pride, fear, and plain stubbornness will keep us plowing on as we are. We would rather trust in our own abilities or just hope that the situation changes. Asking for and depending upon the responses of other people when we're in need don't come easily.

Asking is an intrinsic part of who we are as creatures made by a perfect Creator. We simply haven't been created to be self-sufficient. We cannot meet our own deepest needs (and often struggle to meet the basic ones). We weren't designed to! True life comes in relying on others, and in asking for help. Ultimately, our needs are met by God, the one we were created to depend on, as he responds to our requests in prayer. Even if life doesn't get easier as we learn to pray, we will experience life as God intends. He supplies our needs, and we grow in faith and thankfulness as we learn in Christ to trust in him.

## All Prayer!

Relying on God through prayer isn't a natural instinct, even for believers. In John Bunyan's *The Pilgrim's Progress*, Christian walks through the Valley of the Shadow of Death. Bunyan crafts the scene to teach us that the devil assaults believers with doubts about the certainty of God's love. Christian is tormented. He wields the Sword of the Spirit, but the battle is won as he also takes up what Bunyan calls "All Prayer."[27] The lesson is obvious, that we must go to war against the evil one with both weapons— and in some situations it's All Prayer, which will ultimately bring us the victory. Ask any experienced believer, and we're sure he or she will tell you how true Bunyan's picture is. God delivers us through prayer.

Prayer of course has many dimensions. In prayer we adore and lose ourselves in the wonder of God's attributes, reveling in his sovereign wisdom over all things and in his meticulous care for our various situations. We praise him for the grace he shows us each day. We confess our sins and search our hearts as we seek forgiveness. For Christians in the pressures of daily discipleship, though, prayer is chiefly asking. As we grow in our faith, we ask more and more. Maybe that's not what we might expect, but it's the experience of every maturing Christian. We learn to depend on our loving heavenly Father, and we learn to love that dependence, as we see his good hand in our lives.

Christians are people who stand firm in the life of faith precisely as they pray and as God answers their prayers. Life teaches us that our own resources (any wisdom, talents, or experiences we flatter ourselves we have) simply aren't enough. We need to ask for grace each moment and to discover it. When Paul says "stand," there are no subclauses. He doesn't say, "But if work gets too much, or if there's a pandemic, or if you have money troubles, health troubles, or you're lonely and frustrated, then you have my permission to collapse." We all wobble, and at times all of us fall over. We give in to fear, anger, hopelessness, prayerlessness—but have we got up? Are we standing today? And will we stand, when those temptations and pressures come again? What we do with the weapon of prayer will be the difference between standing and falling. It is literally the difference between our fragile strength and divine omnipotence.

Prayer is the final item in Paul's list of armor and weapons. (Of course, it doesn't really matter if it's a weapon or if it's armor—and matters even less if we fail to pray at all.) Although it's the last named, prayer is not the afterthought in Paul's list but the most important item. We must never treat prayer as a last resort. Staying with his soldier image, we might look good and feel really confident, all dressed for action as we fix our hope again on God's mercies in the gospel and fill our minds with his promises; but if God doesn't go with us into the battle, if he's not with us when things get really tough, will we fight, and will we stand?

## The Man of Prayer Makes a People of Prayer

When it comes to prayer, as with everything else, Jesus is our great example. Jesus prayed. The Son of God, filled with the Holy Spirit, sinless, matchless, marked out by God "with mighty works and wonders and signs that God did through him in your midst" (Acts 2:22), was mighty only through his moment-by-moment reliance on his Father. Magnificence through dependence, we might say. At each key stage of his life, Jesus devoted himself to prayer. He sought the will of his Father in heaven and relied on his guidance and strength. Before his public ministry, at the calling of the disciples, and when exhausted with the demands of serving others, he gave himself to prayer (Matt. 4:1–11; 14:23; Mark 1:35). The shadow of the cross found Jesus in prayer, as he lifted his heart to God on the night of his betrayal and arrest, committing his ministry, his followers, and the completion of his work to his Father (John 17). Then, in the garden of Gethsemane, almost overwhelmed by the full horror of his coming sacrifice, he prayed with tears and cries (Matt. 26:36–46; compare with Heb. 5:7). Jesus, God's beloved Son and perfect servant, was a man of constant prayer. We might say that prayer carried him all the way through the course of his obedience to the Father, until he came to the cross. Even there he prayed (Matt. 27:46; Luke 23:46). His prayers cannot be separated from his obedience, they are an essential part of it. Through prayer he achieved our salvation!

A praying Savior and Lord is the shepherd of a praying people. Jesus's first followers did eventually get the message. Each of those men were at different times hot-headed, proud, and confident in their own gifts before the Lord showed them themselves and their need of grace. Jesus had taught them to pray and modeled it, and they did in time realize that prayer is a vital component of Christian living. Peter saw prayer as absolutely essential for the struggling Christians he wrote to: when trials could make them lose perspective and give way to prayerlessness, he says, "Be self-controlled and sober-minded for the sake of your prayers" (1 Pet. 4:7; compare 4:19; 5:7). James warns believers, "You do not have, because you do not ask" (James 4:2), and both James and John call any with struggles to commit themselves to prayer (James 5:13–16; 1 John 5:16). Paul urges the Colossians, "Continue steadfastly in prayer, being watchful in it with thanksgiving" (Col. 4:2). "Pray without ceasing" is his command to the Thessalonians (1 Thess. 5:17). Each of those disciples embraced risk, danger, and death itself in their calling: God kept them standing until the end because they relied on him. He longs to do just the same for us.

## So Then?

What the nineteenth century preacher Charles Spurgeon said about prayer is so insightful: "I cannot help praying. Prayer has become as essential to me as the filling of my lungs and the beating of my heart."[28] Laying out his needs before God and leaning into the grace supplied in God's answers were absolutely vital to Spurgeon. Read any biography of the man, and you will be stunned at how hard he worked, how much opposition he endured in his loyalty to Christ, and the massive suffering he experienced—particularly in the crippling depression that he battled with for large periods of his adult life. Trials compelled Spurgeon to live close to his Lord. The Lord never failed him. Not once. Nor will he fail you, as you lean on him.

"Lord, teach us to pray" (Luke 11:1). And we long for him to do that for all of us. The Lord's Prayer gives us a lesson on the priorities for our prayers—how to worship and confess and what to pray for (vv. 2–4). He also teaches us to pray as he leads us in life and gently allows life to be overwhelming, its demands swamping the little boat of our own resources and faith. Then we go to him in our struggles, and we cast ourselves on him. We're desperate, because we can't do it on our own. And so, we pray.

He hears, and he answers. The storms of life quite often don't stop, and sometimes get worse, but we know that he is with us, and he gives us strength (compare Paul's experience, as people and their help vanish but the Lord's presence and grace are unfailing, in 2 Tim. 4:16–17). We will be resilient Christians if we learn to seek and then rely on God's fabulous grace in prayer. So will you?

### Reflect

1. Could you identify (and maybe write down) the things that are really causing you stress at the moment? Are you praying about them? Do you believe that the Lord loves to help you in those areas of your life right now?

2. "Cast all your anxiety on him because he cares for you" (1 Pet. 5:7 NIV). How could you do that more often? Is there anything you distrust deep down about the Lord's care and power? Or do you actually trust too much in your own strength?

3. Depending is strengthening for Christians. Spend some time worshiping God, thanking him that he walks through life with you and delights to help you and make you strong at every step as you depend on him.

## Pray

*Lord, I confess that so often I love to think that I'm in charge of my life, and that so often I shy away from you, even when life is hard. Lots of the time I hardly pray, and sometimes I don't pray at all. Forgive me my pride and my lack of faith and my lack of prayer.*

*Help! Help me see how much I need you, and how you want to draw me close to rely on you. Teach me to cast all of my troubles on you and to enjoy this life of trusting, depending prayer. Amen.*

# 21

# The Weak and the Strong

## How Grace Changes a Praying Heart

*. . . making supplication for all the saints.*

EPHESIANS 6:18

MICK IS A FIGHTER. Not with fists and feet and not even with words, but life is a battle for Mick. No one will fight it for him, so Mick set himself to fight the world, the flesh, and the devil. He has no time for weakness, and little time for weak people as he sees them.

Mick's also a Christian. He was pretty lukewarm about church growing up ("Those people! And those cringey youth programs!"), but a decisive encounter with Jesus at college really turned him around. For the first time Mick understood the gospel and felt its power, and he knew instantly that he had something to live for. Now he's three years into his first job and the church in his new town, and he's starting to find his way. That's what he thinks.

It's just that it's a frustrating way. Everyone seems to Mick to be so lukewarm. After an exhausting day at work he takes himself off to the Bible study group, and he leaves often even more weary. Mick contributes to the studies, but he sometimes grits his teeth at the silences or the half-hearted offerings of others. Prayer requests seem to Mick to be lame excuses for uncommitted discipleship. He doesn't want to hear about people's aches and pains or their hard time with a sister or a boss. *Haven't they got any* real *problems or serious ambitions for the Lord?* Mick wonders. Inwardly he sighs at what he hears. *Why aren't these guys forging ahead for the kingdom?* he asks himself. *Where's the courage?* he wonders.

Mick doesn't realize it yet, but unless he can align his passion for the Lord with a passionate—and patient—love for people, he's never going to grow as a strong Christian. And he might miss the way altogether. What passes as zeal, if it's not shaped and sustained by love, could end in disaster. Mick needs to grow in love for others, expressed in committed prayer for them. We all face the challenge too. Strong discipleship means patient, praying love for people. Without that, we are dangerously weak.

## Love-Fueled Prayer

Ephesians 6:18 instructs Christians to be "making supplication for all the saints." Some of us excel at this. Some have people on their hearts all the time, they feel that it's a privilege to pray for others and to see the Lord at work in others' lives. Then some might want to develop a personal ministry of intercession for others, but they've just never started. They can't really see how they ever will, and they are secretly resigned to staying as they are. Praying for others is one of the true signs of a growing Christian, and we all need to grow in this area.

Serving others with prayer is a deeply authentic way of loving them. The Christian life is a shared life. The Bible often speaks of Christians as saints, but it never speaks of an individual saint. God's vision is to save individuals, but then he makes communities out of them, each having a place and a part. We are God's people, together. So we pray for one another, and we pray together.

That's why in our church, we have our life groups (sometimes called small groups in other churches). Life groups meet each week so that we can share God's word, share our lives, and share joys and sorrows as we pray for each other in a smaller, tighter knit community. We also make a monthly time to meet as a whole church family and give that time exclusively to prayer. It's vital that we lift our voices together in prayer and give ourselves to seeking the Lord together.

## Strategic Prayer

" . . . and also for me" (Eph. 6:19). When do you stop needing prayer? When can you stop praying, and asking others to pray for you? The answer is . . . death! In other words, we always, always need prayer, and if we are wise we will ask for prayer from others regularly. A mature Christian knows his weaknesses and asks for prayer from others. If Paul needed prayer, and asked for it, then his example must burn itself on our hearts.

Notice, Paul asks that fellow Christians pray that he would share the gospel. Gospel preaching was his controlling ambition (Acts 20:24; Rom. 1:14–15; 1 Cor. 9:16), and for it he needed all of God's help. In himself, Paul knows that he's not got the resources to do it. Seasoned apostle and preacher though he was, Paul knew the temptation to be fearful in the face of his commission. Twice he requests prayer support so that he will preach the gospel "boldly" (Eph. 6:19–20). Charles Hodge makes this comment on the passage: "It is not armour or weapons which make the warrior. There must be courage and strength—and even then he often needs help. As the Christian has no strength in himself, and can succeed only as aided from above, the apostle urges the duty of prayer."[29] Knowing your weaknesses, and getting others to pray about them, is a sure sign of being a growing Christian. You just can't manage the Christian life on your own. You need the Lord, and in him you need other people and their prayers. Likewise, they need your prayers and your encouragement. That is how grace works.

## The Weak Made Strong

Let's get back to Mick, then, and see how his story turned out. Mick made a secret deal with himself. He told himself that if his Bible study members didn't change and grow, he would leave the group and find a different group that provided more encouragement. He gave them three months to change, though he didn't really think anything would happen. Three months, he thought to himself, and he would be free!

Once Mick had made his decision, he thought he should perhaps pray for them, say, just once a week. He did. After that first week, he actually thought he could maybe pray for two members of the group each day, and work through the whole group each week in his prayers. He did. What happened next bewildered Mick. A month into his new prayer habit, he noticed that his attitude was changing toward the group members. The weekly meeting still felt like hard work, but Mick knew that his heart was in a different place. He wasn't inwardly scolding the wrong answers, groaning at the silences when people avoided contributing, or tutting to himself when they gave vague prayer points or didn't pray out loud. Instead, Mick felt a new respect and compassion for them. He saw more clearly their problems, and he started to feel more deeply for them. He prayed for God to work in their lives, and found that God was working in him too. Weak love was finding strength all by God's grace.

Actually, Mick saw real change in his Bible study group, just as its members saw change in Mick. Together, they became more open and confident to share their struggles and to ask each other for help. Strangers were becoming friends. Christ was being treasured and glorified. And this was because of the struggles of one person's heart.

Like all of us, Mick still has a long way to go. He still has an instinct to push away other Christians whom he finds difficult, and he often needs to check an impatient spirit. Mick is learning what all of us who wish to be strong in the Lord need to learn: God is challenging us to humble ourselves to serve others, which includes loving them through a ministry of prayer. We walk with them and bear their burdens and bring their problems, gifts, situations, and needs to the Lord for him to work in. That is love.

Persevering in loving the saints in prayer, through weeks, months, and maybe many years, is a deep expression of love for them and for our shared Savior.

For this we need grace, and in this we find glory!

### Reflect

1. Have you developed some consistent habits of intentional daily praying yet? What steps could you take to start (or refresh) your prayer habits?

2. Thank the Lord for the fellow Christians he has put in your life. Take time to do this and notice the different signs of God's grace in their lives.

3. Are any of your Christian friends causing you stress? Are you praying for them? Why not commit to regular prayer for them? Look for answered prayer in their lives as you do—but don't be surprised if the biggest change is actually in your heart.

### Pray

*Lord, forgive me when I often just try to do my own thing and hold other people at arm's length. I get impatient with others, and I don't want to enter into other people's lives, or open my life to them.*

*Forgive me, Father, when I try and hold you at arm's length. I can be so reluctant to pray.*

*Please open my heart with a deeper love for the people you've put in my life. Make me a true friend to them as you lead me on a journey of prayer for their needs too. Amen.*

22

# The Spirit Is Here

Experiencing the Spirit as We Pray

*Continue steadfastly in prayer.*

COLOSSIANS 4:2

MAYBE YOU'VE PUZZLED over Paul's phrase, "Praying . . . in the Spirit" (Eph. 6:18)? Many have. "Praying in the Spirit" sounds effort-free, spontaneous, exciting, and liberating. What a disconnect (or, a deliverance!) from the life of intentional and disciplined praying, with its reminders, routines, and effort. Isn't the Spirit the wings to lift us above the labor of prayer, the battle to concentrate and to believe?

No. When we are praying in the Spirit, we are being obedient to what the Spirit desires, and bringing those desires to God in prayer. To be obedient to what the Spirit desires involves discovering a struggle between the Spirit and what we in our sluggish and sinful natures still desire—to prioritize ourselves and rely on our own resources. When the Spirit is at work, he is driving us to Jesus, to his kingdom priorities, and to care about and pray for what he wants. The Spirit drives us out of ourselves, into a deepening love for Jesus, and into a world of worship and intercession.

## Spirit-Disciplined Prayer

Spirit-disciplined prayer is what I (Lewis) saw in Ellen's life. Ellen wanted to be married, to have a job that was rewarding without being all-consuming, to be happily involved in church, and to keep up with friends and family. The Spirit, though, didn't want to make her dreams come true without also working to change her deep within. He wanted to take her already sensitive and kind heart and really fill it with a fuller love for Christ that would drive her to prayer.

How did he do that? For Ellen, although she got the job and the husband, life began to stutter. Work brought more tears than smiles. Yes, marriage was a gift, but a far more demanding one than she ever thought it would be. Friends couldn't carry her burdens, the church didn't always understand her pressures, and well-meaning family sometimes got things wrong too. Life wasn't going according to her plan.

Her life was, though, going absolutely to God's plan. It seems that heaven was wanting her to discover the Spirit's power, which was leading her to give herself to prayer in a new way. She was starting to pray as a believer who really needed God's grace. As she looked for God's help, she started to see how many signs of his love there were all around her, asked-for signs as well as there-all-the-time signs. Also, the Spirit was opening her eyes to how she could support others and really serve them in practical ways. Her pain, in other words, was opening her to the Lord and to others, to rely on him, and to give herself for him. It was hard, but Ellen's faith was being steadily deepened, and she was putting it to work in a ministry of prayer and service for others.

When we pray in the Spirit, we're deliberately seeking to live under the lordship of Christ. We submit to his reign in our hearts. When we do that, we discover that God is at work, weaning us off our worldly desires and fixing us on what he wants. It is a struggle, just as we all know how hard it is to leave behind habits of thinking and behavior. The struggle, though, is one the Spirit is invested in. Prayer isn't the final piece in an otherwise full and rewarding life, when we spare an afterthought for the Lord and his kingdom. Equally, it's more than the agonized cry when life goes wrong and we're finally "cornered" and need to talk to God. It's the centerpiece of life as God is leading and arranging it. A praying life isn't a charmed, pain-free life, but it is a life where Jesus is making himself known in the pain and working out the glories of his love through his Spirit.

## Vigilant Prayer

One of the Roman poets of Paul's day famously said, "Every lover is a fighter."[30] Love has enemies, obstacles, and opposition as it strives to express itself. Jesus fought sin, Satan, death, and hell for his bride, the church. As those who love Jesus, believers find that our enemies are real and daunting. Satan is powerful, and the world is a tough place. Living by faith can be very, very hard. We're all in a spiritual war, and sometimes the biggest battle is in our own hearts, when we are tempted and discouraged. What are we going to do?

"Be alert" is the apostle's command, in Eph 6:18 (NIV). In other words, strive to do the opposite of what we naturally want to do when life is difficult, which is to tune out of spiritual promises and encouragements and to seek the gratification of physical things (screens, food, spending, and so on). Resist and be alert. Fight back, alert to God's promises, and fight back through prayer. Take your needs, and the needs of a broken world, to your heavenly Father as his Spirit prompts you to do so. Watch and pray as Jesus said to his disciples in Gethsemane (Matt. 26:36–46).

**Four-Square Prayer . . .**

Paul longs that Christians really give themselves to prayer. That's what being alert means, and it's crucial that we understand this. Being alert doesn't mean living hyper-aware of any possible danger in life or situation or constantly fearing something terrible will happen. Live like that and we'll just grind ourselves down and certainly lose sight of God's loving kindness. There are times when I (Lewis) have made that mistake, being so aware of problems in my life, family, and church that I've been a bundle of nervous energy, which has exhausted me—and everyone around me! Instead, it's better if we stay alert as we continually speak to our Father in heaven. Four times in Ephesians 6:18, Paul uses the word "all": we pray on *all* occasions, with *all* sorts of prayer, with *all* perseverance, for *all* the saints. We immerse ourselves in prayer, continually bringing people and pressures to God. That is the way to live by faith, as conscious, Spirit-powered effort keeps us looking to Jesus.

Let's get practical and specific now. What might that sort of praying look like in our lives? Let's trace Paul's four prayer priorities:

*All occasions:* That's going to mean moment by moment, as we pray short, focused, and believing prayers. It could be in the car, in the kitchen, as we walk, even in the shower. We pray as we walk the dog, go for a run, take the train or bus to work or college, or do as the last thing at night or first thing in the day.

*All sorts of prayer:* Our prayers can be short ones and long ones, arrow-like prayers in a crisis, slower and more deliberate prayers when we have time to reflect. We intercede for pressing situations, but we also pray strategically into the future for those we love. We pray on the go, but we also make time for focused prayer (more of this in a moment).

*All perseverance:* To get going in prayer can be hard and to keep going can be hard too. But we must! The Spirit fights against our inner unbelief and is always urging us to live by faith not by sight. To persevere in prayer means trusting God. It means we pray again and again and again: sometimes asking for the same things, and at other times adjusting our prayers, as we feel led. But it means to keep on praying. Literally, don't ever stop.

*All the saints:* A Christian loves other Christians, recognizing them all as blood-bought saints and sinners who share the Spirit and call on the same heavenly Father. So we must pray for each other. God's local and worldwide family are calling for our prayers, and desperately need them. Family, friends, church family, struggling saints, the persecuted saints, key ministries bringing grace to others—all need us to get praying and keep on praying. If we're only interceding for people we know, or feel an affinity with, then many are missing out on the grace that the Lord wants to work in response to our prayers. Let's catch that bigger vision of serious "all the saints" prayer.

The example of the apostle Paul is a wonderful challenge. Read the closing chapter of Romans, or the lists of names at the end of 1 Corinthians or Colossians, and it's striking how many people are on Paul's heart. Surely he prayed for them too. In his letters Paul also mentions those he hasn't even met and won't meet till glory; and yet, he still prays for them. Could God so open your heart in love that you learn to care about and intercede for many more than you currently do? Yes, he can. And just imagine the person you could be, set free to serve others with radical love as you intercede for them.

### . . . and Five-Fold Praying

"Continue steadfastly in prayer" (Col. 4:2) is a call to dedicated praying. If you're to grow in your prayer life, enjoying and seeing fruit, you need to devote time to it. That will include making a top priority of establishing a daily time. Best of all is  when you can couple your prayers with your regular time in God's word and allow what he's saying to you to guide your intercessions. There is no substitute for fixing pretty much the same time each day where you can give undistracted focus to praying. For most believers, trial and error suggests that a morning time before things get really busy works best. If you get that habit in place, you will take that spirit of prayer into the day and be much more alert to praying (and to looking for answers to prayer) as you meet the day's challenges.

All of us need a nudge to get going in prayer and to make sure that we're praying widely. Here are five pointers that you could follow. Consider writing out these areas for prayer in your phone or notebook, and then add some names and places under each.

1. Your home or immediate family—Living with others is meant to be a joy, but it's often got many pressure points. Bring those to the Lord in prayer.

2. Your wider family and friends—If you're a believer in a minority among those you love, take up a call to pray for them as your special responsibility. The Lord will honor your prayers. If friends and family are Christians, that's wonderful, but they don't need your prayers any less.

3. Your non-Christian friends and neighbors—Pray for their salvation and for opportunities to share the gospel with them.

4. Your church family, leaders, and ministries—The church is a world of need; don't forget to keep lifting her up in prayer.

5. The world—Why not pray for a country each day and a cross-cultural ministry dear to your heart? Let reading the news become the springboard for worldwide prayer.

## Reflect

1. Have you developed some consistent habits of intentional daily praying yet? What's stopping you (dare to be honest!)?

2. What steps could you take to start (or refresh) your prayer habits?

3. Is there someone you could set up a regular time of prayer with as you grow in your prayer life?

## Pray

*Lord, teach me to trust. Teach me to love. And then, teach me to pray. Turn my heart inside out, move me from love of self to deep concern for others. May your Spirit make me a person who loves you and others so much that I pray for them. Amen.*

# PART 9

# THE CHURCH

Being a pastor means being set apart to love and be loved by the most wonderful community on earth, the servants of Jesus Christ. But what every pastor finds soon enough is that not everyone shares his enthusiasm for the church. In fact, for a lot of Christians, coming to worship, getting to know others, and getting involved in fellowship are the last things they want to do. Sure, many believers have been hurt by people or ministries in the past and the temptation to withdraw can be so attractive. Why face more pain?

That's a good question. The simple truth is that, imperfect as every church is and terrible as some experiences of Christians can be, every believer is commanded by God to gather in the church to worship, fellowship, and serve. If we are to keep enjoying our union with Christ, we must reckon with the priorities of gathering with brothers and sisters for weekly worship and of finding a meaningful place among them. Of course, involvement brings its demands (what relationships don't?), but the Spirit helps us dig in.

So, in our final part we're looking at God's great plan for us as his people, to pursue him together. First, there is the call of God to all believers to worship together. It's in worship that the Lord comes to his people and lifts their hearts to himself. Let's study and savor that truth. Then, God's people are to heed the command to love one another. That can only be done where there are meaningful relationships, so we'll be looking at how we need to work on our attitudes and our habits in order to grow together. Finally, we acknowledge that our Lord has equipped us to serve one another. Everyone has gifts, all are empowered to serve. We take an honest look at why people find it hard to give themselves for others, but we'll be having a sight of the glories of serving too.

All of this is designed to get us excited about the church again and confident that she is the core way in which we will learn together to be resilient Christians, standing together in Christ.

23

# Sharing Worship

## The Church Meets Her Lord

*Because your steadfast love is better than life,*
*my lips will praise you.*

PSALM 63:3

THE HARDEST THING for struggling Christians to recognize is that church is exactly the community they need. So often, they feel it isn't. Church, they tell themselves, is for the strong, the confident, the "at peace with God and man" believers. When Christians who are finding the journey hard really need to be part of the church, they convince themselves they should be anywhere but church.

## The Weary Go to Worship

Is it the tempter at work, or is it just the natural instincts of discouraged people to isolate themselves? It's both, of course. But this can't be the final answer for exhausted saints. All Christians always need one another. The church is God's masterpiece, the community in which his glory in Jesus is displayed (John 17:22; 2 Cor. 3:18). If we're struggling in our faith, we simply need to get ourselves to that glory display.

David knew this, as Psalm 63 testifies. The harsh desert he found himself in was a stark picture of his life, the life he had so nearly destroyed. Despite all of his sin, and the utter despair he could have been swallowed up by (his own son was hunting him down), David knew he was utterly secure in God's covenant love. He encouraged his heart by thinking back to precious worship in the sanctuary, the place where he had gazed on God's power and glory (Ps. 63:2). His testimony in all of his personal turmoil? "Your steadfast love is better than life" (v. 3). It is. And it's in the worship of Jesus Christ with others that we uniquely behold the power and glory of God's grace.

We see glory in the gathering of the church. As Christians come to worship, God comes to meet with his people. We both really do mean that. Years of church involvement can lead us all to be sceptics. We all are skilled at detecting insincerity, mixed motives, fixed smiles hiding pain or sin (most likely both). We all inwardly groan at clumsy leading, bad music, and bad preaching. Maybe some are dealing with wounds of unkindness from leaders and people alike. Sundays can be stressful. This much is true.

What is truer still, amid the failure, is that Jesus comes to shepherd his people. Sunday by Sunday, as we sing, pray, hear preaching, celebrate baptism and the Lord's Supper, and open our lives to one another, we encounter the glorious love of the Good Shepherd by his Spirit. The Lord who has died to win his church to himself delights to walk in her midst. There is a substitute for our isolated struggles, and it is the corporate gathering of the church. The weary need to hear this and believe it.

How are you doing? Do you get up on a Sunday morning with a "shall I, shan't I?" dilemma, ready to make up your mind about church according to whether you're feeling good about the faith or about yourself? How about instead, you get up, whether with a joyful or a heavy heart, and tell yourself, *Jesus is calling me to assemble with the saints. He wants me to draw close to him with others and to refresh and help me. He wants to use me to bring encouragement to fellow strugglers. This is my privilege and my duty.* You worship, because he is worthy and because you need to be a worshiper. Worship nurtures faith.

## Worship—but Not as We Know It?

In some circles it's been fashionable to downgrade the place of the weekly worship gathering. The reasoning is that God wants all of our lives to be worship, as he has redeemed every area to be filled with his praise and service. After all, doesn't Paul tell us that, whatever we do, we are to do it "to the glory of God" (1 Cor. 10:31)? Surely, then, worship can be working, golfing, traveling, sleeping in, and everything else besides? So let's not lift the Sunday experience higher than the Bible does, or so goes the popular wisdom.

Some might say, "But how much do you worship God when you focus on the golf ball? How conscious are you of the Lord and his goodness, and happily responding to him in thanksgiving when you're navigating a stressful relationship at work?" Yes, these are real areas for you to develop your awareness of the Lord and satisfaction in him; but worship is a conscious, intentional bringing of mind, heart, and body to the Lord as we praise, thank, pray to, listen to, and enjoy him.

That's what the Bible teaches us in both Testaments. In the vast majority of its uses, the main word for "worship" in the New Testament speaks of the church on earth and in heaven praising and adoring God together (see Matt. 14:33; 28:17; Acts 13:2; Rev. 4:10; 5:13–14; 19:4). It is something Christians stop everything else in order to do. We turn aside from the good (enjoying God in all of his gifts) to focus on the best (enjoying conscious fellowship with him in the gathering and shared worship of fellow believers).

This worship strengthens faith. We worship, and our faith is deepened. We don't wait until we have deep faith before we worship God. We take the little we believe, the little we know, the thanks and the praise we have—aware that it feels so little—and we bring it to him. And he meets us.

**Worship Rules!**

If Sunday worship is this important and faith-building event, let's take a few basic pointers for really engaging in it in ways that bring blessings. Here are four for you:

*1. Come expectantly.* That means you will pray. Pray for your heart, for all of our hearts. Each Sunday morning in my quiet time I (Lewis) try to pray for the discouraged, the weary, and the unsaved—I sort of figure that that covers most of the people at church! I'm aware that there are many vibrant and joyful saints, but I'm aware too that almost every heart carries deep sorrows, and

I long that all meet their comforting God in Christ. I'm praying, and therefore expecting, that he will meet with them.

Do you pray before you come to church? What do you pray for? And do you pray that the good shepherd would call his sheep, feed them, strengthen and reassure their hearts, and strengthen them to love and serve him? Pray for the preaching, for those who lead worship, for those who teach children, and for those who welcome and serve in many other ways. Pray that all in the congregation would experience and enjoy grace. Expect the Lord to work and show that expectation as you pray.

*2. Come to encourage.* We encourage when we come on time. All of us are late sometimes, but none of us should be late all the time or even most of the time. That is distracting and discouraging to others. If gathered worship is what the Bible says it is, the coming of Jesus to his people and his people to Jesus, then we come ready to meet the King, and we come on time.

*3. Come to take part.* We are all called to worship. None of us are passengers, spectators, or critics. So sing wholeheartedly, pray with focus, listen with care. Worship is an act of mind, heart, and body. Yes, body too. Stay focused—raise your voice. If you want to raise your hands, raise your hands. But for your sake, and for your Master's honor, don't be a half-hearted worshiper. Worship is Christians delighting in God's love in Christ, and bringing all that we are, with our thanks, our praise, as well as our struggles and needs, and eagerly coming into God's presence to find his love and strength for us. Wholehearted worshipers encourage and spur on others.

*4. Come to share with others.* It makes no difference if you're not at the front, this week or any week. We are all sharers. We all come to encourage, to welcome, to help, and to serve. No one comes without something to share. We come to praise; we also come to get to know others and share burdens. Where else do we want to be? This is our family. This is the church of the living God.

**Reflect**

1. Spend some time thanking the Lord for the gift of church and its ministry. Repent of bad attitudes to church. Be honest with him about where church is hard for you and pray for grace to love and serve in your church.

2. How does corporate worship build your faith? Reflect on, say, the worship services of the last two months at your church. How have they grown your faith in and love for Jesus?

3. How can you get more out of Sunday worship? And are there ways you could contribute more to encourage others?

## Pray

*Lord Jesus, thank you that you love your body, the church. You are committed to her. Please forgive me when I want to push your church away and fail to value its gatherings as I should. Renew my heart in thankfulness and love for your people and ignite my passion to worship you with my brothers and sisters. For your sake, Lord Jesus, amen.*

24

# Leaning In

Enjoying Family Life Together

*Now you are the body of Christ,*
*and each one of you is a part of it.*
I CORINTHIANS 12:27 NIV

MY FRIEND JULIE was going through a really difficult patch in her family life. She explained it to her life group and asked them to pray. On the next Sunday morning, Julie was greeted by one of the group members. "I've been praying for you," he said loudly. "How are things going with . . . ?", and then he proceeded to give her ten minutes of not very helpful advice which half the church could hear.

Julie was furious. You would be too, wouldn't you? Julie said to me, "Why can Christians be so insensitive? My non-Christian friends behave better!"

It's probably true. Julie is a sensitive and thoughtful woman, and her friends are like her. Like attracts like in friendship circles. We all hang out with people who are like us, because that makes life easy. Not so at church. Church is the place where we meet all sorts of people, and many of them just aren't a bit like us. Only the gospel calls us together—and can keep us together.

## You Choose Your Friends, but Not Your Family

Any true church is a bewildering mix of people. There are older folk, youngsters, people who left school with few qualifications, and those with a handful of degrees. Some have been born and bred in the area, others have lived in two or more continents. A good number have had a comfortable life so far, but there are also quite a few who have been deeply impacted by addictions and relationship breakdown. Some have great social skills, others lack them, as Julie found out. To be honest, lots probably wouldn't choose each other as friends, that is, if we weren't Christians. It would be too much hard work.

God has chosen every believer to be in his family. He has chosen us not just for himself, but for each other. Paul tells the Corinthian church that "the body is one and has many members" (1 Cor. 12:12), and goes on to explain how, just as a human body functions with many different parts, so does the church. "The eye cannot say to the hand, 'I have no need of you,' nor again the head to the feet, 'I have no need of you'" (v. 21). All parts are needed, and all parts are valuable. In fact, the church isn't just *like* a body, we *are* Christ's body. All Christians around the world and through the ages make up the body of Christ, the universal church. Local congregations operate the same way, as a body, with different parts working together in love for the common good.

When we meet people not like us, and difficult people in particular, it is tempting to think that they are the problem. If only they were like me, we reckon, then everything would be easy! God really needs to grow them in godliness, we decide, as we withdraw and judge from a distance. How terrible of us. Who do we think we are?

Whether or not we've got a true picture of someone else's spiritual state (and most often we don't) withdrawal won't help them or us. People change through love, and love reaches out. Jesus came close to sinners and ate with them. He comes to me in my sin, as well as the difficult person over there in her sin. So now we can move toward each other with his love. This is church.

It isn't easy, that's for sure. Plenty of us are introverts and feel much happier talking to those we already know. But if you want to learn to be more like Jesus, this is surely one of the best ways— you just need to go outside of your comfort zone. Get up out of your seat or pick up your phone; make the first move and reach out in love to someone not like you. Perhaps you'll discover that you need to change more than they do. Maybe you'll learn that all along you're the difficult one, and that God is bringing you alongside someone to help you to change.

## Called Together to Grow Together

Julie's experience of that uncomfortable conversation came because she had been sharing a need. In her really painful difficulty, she had done what is normal for Christians and asked for prayer. She might have felt that some of her secular friends would have listened better, and offered better advice, but her Christian friends prayed, and so ultimately, they offered the best help of all.

Being really honest with our brothers and sisters can feel like a risk, if we don't know what reception we'll get. Being open can make us seem weak and dependent. That, of course, is what we are. Paul's image of the body is of a collection of parts that cannot operate alone. We depend on our head, Christ, first and foremost, and we depend on each other too. In fact, being a foot has no usefulness or meaning apart from a leg, and a nose is pointless without a throat. The greatest pioneering missionary depends on prayerful supporters and the best published theologian relies on his small church pastor's preaching.

Our dependence on each other binds us together. Peter writes, "Like living stones, [you] are being built into a spiritual house to be a holy priesthood, offering spiritual sacrifices acceptable to God through Jesus Christ" (1 Pet. 2:5 NIV). Each stone is placed on others, and in turn supports more stones. Our dependence on each other, and through each other on Christ, should result in a precious unity. When united, the church can serve God.

If we treat church as a means to meet our needs, or as a comfortable community network, a kind of religious neighborhood watch, then we perhaps shouldn't be surprised that it is quite a dull place, where people drift in and out. If we catch Peter's vision for a church of unity, holy dependence, and Jesus-focused sacrifice, then church will be a very different place. Church begins to be demanding, but glorious. Jesus is at work.

Maybe you've had the experience of working in a short-term mission or on a Bible camp team. For a week or two, focused on a single common goal, people can work together brilliantly. The experience is normally exhausting, but exhilarating when we see the creativity, devotion, and kindness of our teammates. That kind of full-on focus can't be replicated in the long-term, week-to-week ministry of the church for all kinds of reasons, but imagine—what if something of that atmosphere of unity in service could be found in your small group or your congregation?

What might need to change in you for that to happen?

There could be more honesty about your needs and greater commitment in responding to needs in your group. When someone shares a concern with you, what do you do? Do you pray there and then with them? Perhaps. Will you remember that prayer need during the week? Will you follow it up with a card or text to let them know you are praying? Could you offer to meet to pray and talk again—and really do it?

There could be practical help offered and accepted. When someone confesses he or she is exhausted or lonely or stretched, what might you do? Make a meal, baby-sit, offer financial support?

There could be willingness to serve beyond the church together. Can you work together in your community? Pray frequently and with knowledge for the local area? Plan and do the hard work of going out to get to know non-Christians and sharing the gospel with them?

## Love That Shines

Before I (Lewis) became a Christian, I met a group of students. They were all so different from each other that it was really odd seeing them in a room together. One was sporty, another artistic, a couple were highly academic, and some of them were definitely not at all cool. What was even stranger to me was that they really seemed to care for each other. I'd never seen a group of people like this College Christian Union before, and this strangeness got me thinking about the God they spoke about.

The sheer diversity of the local church is part of God's plan for the salvation of the world. From the earliest chapters of the Bible, we see the Lord drawing unexpected individuals into his one nation. There were Egyptians who joined the Hebrews to journey to the promised land, Ruth the Moabite who became a great-grandmother of Jesus, and the Babylonian King Nebuchadnezzar who acknowledged that Yahweh is God of all (Ex. 12:38; Matt. 1:5–6; Dan. 4:37). They are just the foretaste of the age we live in now, when all nations are being drawn to worship Jesus. God wants diversity in his church, different kinds of people who are deeply committed to each other. This kind of variety is a bright light, a revelation of God's powerful love, drawing even more people to him. The apostle John makes this extraordinary claim: "No one has ever seen God; but if we love one another, God lives in us and his love is made complete in us" (1 John 4:12 NIV).

The churches John knew were made up of all kinds of groups. There were slaves and slave owners, Gentiles and Jews, and we know that there were tensions between these groups, which needed intervention (e.g., Acts 6:1–4). The answer wasn't to keep them apart, instead it was for them to grow in love and in self-denial. Then as now, careful thought and strategy were needed from the leaders, and at times mediation was required to maintain unity (Phil. 4:2; Philem. 17). Formal church discipline sometimes had to take place where division was caused by a refusal to repent (1 Tim. 1:20).

It takes effort to be part of a united, loving church, and when life is hard, that might feel too much. It needs the effort of hospitality and awkward conversations or laborious self-denying service.

We just can't keep going as resilient Christians on our own. We have been made and saved for fellowship. To know Jesus is to be part of his body, it is to be dependent on others, and to know they depend on us. Commit to your family and you are committing to growing more like Jesus.

### Reflect

1. Which part of fellowship in your local church do you particularly value? Which do you find more difficult? Why might that be?

2. Meditate on this verse, considering what each description of the church highlights about our relationship with God and each other:

   But you are a chosen people, a royal priesthood, a holy nation, God's special possession, that you may declare the praises of him who called you out of darkness into his wonderful light. (1 Pet. 2:9 NIV)

3. What one part of life together can you work on this week? Is there one thing you can start doing that can help you love your brothers and sisters more? Write it down and act on it!

## Pray

*Dear Lord Jesus, I thank you that the church is your possession, however messy and painful it sometimes is. Help me to remember your headship when I am tempted to despair or withdraw, and show me how I might better live in love with my brothers and sisters this week. Lord, give me opportunities to work for unity in the church and to declare your wonderful praises to this dark world for the glory of the Father, amen.*

# 25

# Resilient through Serving

## The Spirit Sustains and Grows Jesus's Servants

*I pray that the sharing of your faith may become*
*effective for the full knowledge of every good*
*thing that is in us for the sake of Christ.*

PHILEMON 6

THE CHURCH, as we've been thinking, is people. Its Bible ministry, its outreach, its worship services, sacraments, organization, and structures all exist in order to serve people. We have all been given the Holy Spirit in order to build one another up (1 Cor. 12:7). Even the most struggling believers are equipped and called to serve. In fact, it is through serving that our faith is strengthened. That is why serving is a vital part of a resilient faith, and why we must resist the temptation to avoid being committed to the church when life is hard.

## For Pete's Sake

Pete caused his church leaders to scratch their heads—a lot. They wanted to be really sensitive to his depression. They were flexible and patient when he felt so low that he couldn't get himself to church or couldn't be relied on to do his duties in the children's ministry. There was a lot of prayer for Pete, and a lot of encouragement given. When Pete didn't show, his leaders often inquired where he was, but they didn't think it was their place to urge him, dependent upon God's grace, to drag himself to church and to stay involved. Which means that what Pete didn't get was a gentle encouragement to stay committed to his ministry as much as he could, so he drifted away from serving, and, in time, Sunday worship became hit and miss. This struggler still had much to give, and also much to receive by keeping at his responsibilities. He needed love, but not a reason to step aside from the work he was doing for the Lord.

If we're going to keep going in our faith, we need help to keep serving.

Serving is a privilege, as well as a place for growth, for all of us. The apostle Paul wrote to his friend Philemon, asking him to step out in his discipleship in ways that were costly and maybe personally humiliating for Philemon. Paul did so with this encouragement: "I pray that the sharing of your faith may become effective for the full knowledge of every good thing that is in us for the sake of Christ" (Philem. 6). The sharing here is not evangelism, but a radically generous forgiveness forged in gospel faith, in order to bless a needy brother (in this case, the slave who had deserted Philemon). As Philemon knew, the call of Christ is often a hard one; Paul's encouragement is that with costly service comes the deepening awareness that we serve a wonderful God who has given us every good thing in Christ. As we sacrifice in love for others, we appreciate more and more the sacrifice of our Savior for us.

**So How Do We Serve?**

Here are three pointers:

*1. Humility, Not Self-Importance*

We need humility before Jesus, our great Redeemer and King. It also means humility before others. To the disciples, convinced of their all-round brilliance and importance, Jesus said. "If anyone would be first, he must be last of all and servant of all" (Mark 9:35). This stunning command rocks our proud hearts. Can we? Will we?

So the next time that difficult person calls you—well, your heart might not leap for joy, but don't dare to think, "I'm too important for you, don't waste my time." No, our time is other people's time, and we're not too important for anyone. When you're approached yet again by someone in church desperately trying to fill the roster for a job everyone else wants to avoid, be careful about automatically avoiding it. Our calling is to live humbly and love deeply, giving ourselves to the needs of others.

We must learn to see service as a privilege, not as a burden. Then we will start to grow closer to one another, and learn to honor one another. And Christ will be honored in our midst.

*2. Generosity, Not Self-Centeredness*

God has gifted you to serve and has the power through his Holy Spirit to make that service effective. As we all know, our struggling days are the ones when we're tempted to feel that we haven't been gifted, or don't need to serve. Of course, it's a real fight to keep playing our part when we feel so weak in faith. When these times come your way, you need to keep reminding yourself that the Lord is with you and wants to use you for the sake of others. You must battle not to disappear into yourself, but keep looking outward, with the Lord's help, to the needs of others. Pray for a generous heart and push back against the instinct just to focus on yourself (see Phil. 2:21).

How do you stay generous to others? You gaze at Jesus and allow his generous and totally sacrificial love for you to move you to your core. You spend unhurried time, intentionally focusing on the cross of your Savior. The Spirit will guide your heart and fill it with the love of the Lord.

Why not linger over Augustine's stunning meditation on our Savior's total commitment to us in his death on the cross:

> We gaze on his wounds as he hangs. We see his blood as he dies. We see the price offered by the redeemer, touch the scars of his resurrection. He bows his head, as if to kiss you. His heart is made bare open, as it were, in love to you. His arms are extended that he may embrace you. His whole body is displayed for your redemption. Ponder how great these things are. Let all this be rightly weighed in your mind: as he was once fixed to the cross in every part of his body for you, so he may now be fixed in every part of your soul.[31]

That's it. The Lord who gave all of himself for every part of us can alone lead us away from ourselves into radical generosity. Fix your eyes on him, expect his Spirit to fill you afresh, and allow him to lead you into deeper service.

### 3. Sacrifice, Not Self-Preservation

The way of the cross runs right through the life of the local church. Oh, the world is a hard place to live for Jesus—but don't expect the church to be easy! For all of the delights and comforts of wonderful friendships in the body of Christ, we mustn't kid ourselves that the road will always be smooth. We mustn't think that unless church life is always exciting and appearing fruitful, then something is wrong. Church calls for sacrifice. Selfish desires (which can even include demanding to see the fruit of our labors) must be put to death. There might be lean seasons of service, difficult people to work with, crises, and knockbacks; but Jesus's servants follow the Master in the pattern of his life, and rely on the same Spirit to keep them going.

Of course, there are times when life's struggles mean that it's right we step back from certain ministries for a season. It's certainly never wise to say yes to all that we might do. We are frail servants, not indestructible machines. At the same time, we must be alert to the temptation to protect ourselves from work for the Lord rather than to experience the demands of it. It's in his service that we meet the Savior and are changed to be more like him. What a thrilling prospect!

The Lord will lead you. And he will lead you to express his love. Let's hear Augustine one more time:

What does love look like? It has the hands to help others. It has the feet to hasten to the poor and needy. It has eyes to see misery and want. It has the ears to hear the sighs and sorrows of men. That is what love looks like.[32]

## Remember Pete?

It wasn't a church leader but a friend who asked Pete if he couldn't be more committed to his children's ministry. Pete was irritated at that question. Couldn't everyone see how down he was, how tough life was, how real his depression was? Why should he be expected to serve on top of everything else?

Some more gentle questions from his friend came, and Pete realized that his reasons—although they sounded good—could end up being the reasons why he never did much at all in church despite his own real problems. What's more, they could be the reasons why his faith was standing still and probably going backward. He realized that service made complete sense and could well be a means of spiritual recovery.

So Pete started again and got back to his serving role each Sunday. It was hard. Pete certainly didn't feel he was any good at it or always enjoy it. But the kids there loved it, and their growing faith did stir Pete's heart and challenge his own walk of faith. It was, he concluded, good to serve. Someone had to serve those kids, and the Lord seemed to have decided he was the one. Pete was finding what we all need to discover, that servants grow in the faith and stay in it. May God give us grace to learn the same.

## Reflect

1. We all instinctively hide from the way of the cross with its demands. How are you hiding? Are there difficult people or

challenging tasks? Bring your heart to the Lord. Ask for mercy and grace.

2. Is there a new ministry you might start or a current one to recommit to? Does this need a conversation with a ministry leader to help you get going again?

3. Never forget: the Lord delights in even the smallest things done in his name! Take heart, take small steps, and don't stop—he is with you and for you!

## Pray

*Jesus, your love is amazing. Your commitment to me took you to the cross and the grave. You made yourself nothing and served me totally. You serve me now, strengthening me to follow you. I adore you: Please fill me again with your Spirit and empower me to live out your life, serving gladly to honor you and as I give myself to others. Amen.*

Conclusion

# And So?

JESUS WANTS US to have resilient faith, a faith that relies on him through all of life's trials. If we can get to the end of our life course still trusting and joyfully satisfied in him, then we have lived well. We've brought him glory, and glory awaits us.

We might not set the world alight with our gifts. In fact, we might not even have great gifts, as others might judge them. Our chance to win that children's competition (remember Sarah's success in the introduction?) has been and gone. Maybe, we won't win any of life's prizes. We don't actually need to. Success is standing firm in Christ.

When we stand before him on that day, it will matter little if we've done this or that, achieved our personal goals, got the success we'd hoped for in work or anywhere else. Success is enduring, right until the end, for the Lord. We long to hear him say, "Well done, good and faithful servant" (Matt. 25:21). That will be enough, more than enough.

Until we get there, we have much to do. There are battles to be faced, habits to put into place, patterns of healthy and holy living to work on. There are people to serve and ministries to invest in. There is God's word to know and prayers to pray.

Until we reach the end, there is the Lord himself to know. As Christians growing in a resilient faith, we are keenly aware of how weak we are and how inconsistent. We are learning, though, how strong and faithful Jesus is. We know that he is always totally reliable. We walk through the storms because he walks with us and shields us. We get up tomorrow, because he has walked with us today. As we do, we find that whole years go by, years where his care is so real, his love so complete. We know whom we are trusting. He has not let us down. Because of him, we are standing. "He who began a good work in you will bring it to completion at the day of Jesus Christ" (Phil. 1:6). Faith teaches us to be utterly confident in him, because he really will do it.

# Notes

1. Jess Berthold, "48% of Young Adults Struggled with Mental Health in Mid-2021," University of California San Franscisco, April 13, 2022, https://www.ucsf.edu; Manish Pandey, "Mental Health Negatively Affecting Almost 50% of UK Students in Survey," BBC News, June 29, 2022, https://www.bbc.co.uk; Craig Thorley, "Not By Degrees: Improving Student Mental Health in the UK's Universities," Institute for Public Policy Research, September 2017, https://www.ippr.org/files /2017-09/1504645674_not-by-degrees-170905.pdf.
2. Peter Lewis, *The Glory of Christ* (London: Hodder & Stoughton, 1997), 207.
3. Research shows that going without sleep for just three nights results in anxiety and mood disorders. Regular sleeplessness increases the risk of diabetes, obesity, and high blood pressure. Eric Suni and Alex Dimitriu, "Circadian Rhythm," Sleep Foundation, April 8, 2022, https://www.sleepfoundation.org.
4. William Shakespeare, *Macbeth*, II.ii.34–37.
5. Fred Sanders, "The Theology of Sleep," The Scriptorium Daily, September 6, 2007, https://scriptoriumdaily.com.
6. "When You Believe," performed by Sally Dworsky and Michelle Pfeiffer in *The Prince of Egypt*, directed by Brenda Chapman, Steve Hickner, and Simon Wells (Glendale, CA: DreamWorks, 1998).
7. "The Sands of Time Are Sinking." The words of this old hymn are based on the "Letters of Samuel Rutherford (1600–1661)," from *Immanuel's Land, and Other Pieces* by Anne Ross Cousin (John Nisbet & Co.: London, 1876), 7.

8. Thomas Brooks, "A Serious Discourse Touching a Well-Grounded Assurance," in *The Complete Works of Thomas Brooks* (London: J Nichol, 1866), 2:323.

9. Nancy R. Pearcey, *Love Thy Body* (Grand Rapids, MI: Baker, 2018), 23.

10. It may be that you need to see a specialist who can help with an eating problem. If so, please do reach out urgently to a medical professional and also speak to a trusted friend.

11. "Born to Play" (video), Christians in Sport, January 4, 2016, https://christiansinsport.org.uk.

12. For example, Job and David describe human life as breath (Job 7:16; Ps. 144:4), illustrating its brevity.

13. David Trigg, "Alistair Gordon—Interview: 'For Me, Painting and Faith Are Very Much Intertwined, Like the Warp and Weft of a Tapestry,'" Studio International, September 20, 2021, https://www.studiointernational.com.

14. "Lord's Day 1," Heidelberg Catechism, accessed May 24, 2022, http://www.heidelberg-catechism.com.

15. Angela Duckworth, *Grit* (London: Vermillion, 2017), 264.

16. Terry Mattingly, "Religion: John Wooden, a Faithful Man," *The Seattle Times*, June 10, 2010, https://www.seattletimes.com.

17. John Calvin, *Institutes of the Christian Religion*, ed. John T. McNeill (Philadelphia, PA: Westminster Press, 1967), 1:551 (III.ii.7).

18. J. I. Packer, *Concise Theology* (Leicester, UK: Inter-Varsity Press, 1993), 159.

19. Martin Luther, *Martin Luther: Selections from His Writings*, ed. John Dillenberger (New York: Anchor, 1961), 87.

20. John R. W. Stott, *God's New Society: The Message of Ephesians* (Leicester, UK: Inter-Varsity Press, 1979), 282.

21. T. S. Eliot, *The Complete Poems and Plays* (London: Faber & Faber, 1969), 172.

22. C. S. Lewis, *The Weight of Glory* (San Francisco: Harper One, 2001).

23. Thomas Brooks, *The Works of Thomas Brooks* (Edinburgh: Banner of Truth, 1980), 2:401.

24. "Stand" appears four times in the NIV and three times in the ESV.

25. J. I. Packer, *Keep in Step with the Spirit: Finding Fullness in Our Walk with God* (Wheaton, IL: Crossway, 2021), 134.

26. Martin Luther, quoted in William Hazlitt, *The Table Talk of Martin Luther* (London: H. G. Bohn, 1857), 25.

27. John Bunyan, *The Pilgrim's Progress*, ed. C. J. Lovik (Wheaton, IL: Crossway, 2009), 96.
28. C. H. Spurgeon, *The Metropolitan Park Tabernacle Pulpit* (Pasadena, TX: Pilgrim Publications, 1977), 49:476.
29. Charles Hodge, *A Commentary on Ephesians* (Edinburgh: Banner of Truth, 1991), 288.
30. Ovid, *Amores*, 1.9.
31. Augustine, "On Virginity" GMI 248, quoted in Thomas C. Oden and Christopher A. Hall, *Mark*, Ancient Christian Commentary on Scripture (Downers Grove, IL: Inter-Varsity Press, 1998), 235.
32. Augustine, *Confessions of Saint Augustine* (New York: Bantam Double-day Dell, 1960), 176.

# General Index

Adam, 44, 45, 81, 86, 91, 92, 111, 118
armor (spiritual)
    of avoidance, 116–17
    the belt of truth, 138–39, 163
    of busyness, 117
    of criticism, 116
    of laughter, 116
    of moodiness, 116
    shield of faith, 100, 109
    sword of the Spirit, 161
asking, 169–70
athletes, 85
Augustine, 211, 212–13

Bible, 35, 131–32, 146
    commands in, 99
    daily reading and focus on
        Scripture, 156–57
    five steps to great Bible reading:
        accountable, 150; fight for time,
        149–50; get help, 150; having a
        plan, 150; remember the purpose
        of your reading, 151
    as special, 123–24
body discipline, 87–88
Brooks, Thomas, 67, 133–34
Bunyan, John, 170

Calvin, John, 112
cell growth, 84

Christian ministry, 67
Christians, 13, 15, 78, 91, 104, 109,
        154, 177–78, 191, 192, 196
    as the body of Christ, 201–2
    calling together of, 202-4
    challenges faced by, 4
    daily discipleship, 170–71
    devotion to "do what is good," 95
    and the hope of glorious resurrec-
        tion, 87
    life as a spiritual battle, 4–5
    resiliency, 99, 155, 216
Christians in Sport, 84
church, the, 191–92, 203
    glory in gathering, 194
    as God's masterpiece, 194
    and love, 204–6
    made of people, 208
    and struggling Christians, 193
    See also worship
College Christian Union, 205
COVID-19 pandemic, 1–2
    and restriction of personal freedom, 2
    and UK lockdowns, 77–78
culture creation, 92

David (king of Israel), 135, 194
discipleship, 99, 106, 120
    consistent, 104
    daily effort, 170–71

Easter, 59, 60
Eliot, T. S., 132
England, 109
Eve, 45, 81, 91, 92, 111, 118
Ezekiel, 65

faith, 78, 111, 120, 125, 154, 163, 196
  Bible's teaching concerning, 113
  Calvin's definition of, 112
  growth of, 170–71
  raising of, 111–13
  sharing of, 209
  the shield of, 100, 109
  Spirit-gifted, 112
fear, 169
fellowship, 191, 192
focusing, 48–51
food
  as not an end to itself, 83
  problematic eating, 82–83, 218n10
  satisfaction of, 81–82
  sharing of, 82
  See also God, free feast of
friends, 201–2

God, 104, 120, 128, 145, 146, 158,
    162, 172, 185
  beloved of, 36
  call to us, 95
  expectations for us, 141–42
  faithfulness of, 62
  fights for his people, 119–20
  free feast of, 82–83
  glory of, 65, 111, 157
  grace of through Christ, 44, 46, 65,
    100, 102, 103, 162, 170, 194
  love of, 205
  loving kindness of, 186
  plan for us, 192
  power of, 5, 74, 141, 149
  promises of, 61, 112, 125, 147, 186
  provision of, 5, 26–27, 86
  renews and remakes us, 45
  rest of, 36–38
  as a righteous judge, 111

shaping his creation, 91–92
  truth of, 103, 132, 133, 134–35, 163
  word of, 123–24, 125, 126, 127,
    128, 146, 154–55, 162, 178, 188
gospel, the, 104, 108, 148
  message of, 101–2
  as God's truth, 100
  resiliency of, 99–100
Gurkha regiments, 127

habits, 148–49
Holy Spirit, the, 60, 71–73, 86, 103,
    126, 128–29, 132, 133, 141, 149,
    155, 157–58, 211
  effectiveness of, 62
  fruits of, 72–73
  praying in, 183–84
  reliance upon, 161–62
  sword of the Spirit, 161
hope, 55–56, 57
  for the future, 66–68
  in Jesus, 65–66
  real, 73–75
  and the Spirit, 71–73
hormonal highs, 84
humility, 22, 157, 210

Isaiah, 61
Israelites, 145

James, on prayer, 173
Jesus Christ, 8, 14, 71, 86, 94, 104,
    111, 117, 127–28, 145, 146, 148,
    155–56, 158, 162, 172, 211–12
  body of, 201–2
  closeness to sinners, 202
  death of, 59–60
  devotion to prayer, 172
  faithfulness of, 216
  final salvation in, 100
  first followers of, 172–73
  as the founder and protector of our
    faith, 113
  as heaven's glorious hope, 65–66
  fighting our battles, 117–19

as Lord of the Sabbath, 37
lordship of, 185
loving embrace of, 13, 139
as a man, 87–88
as representative of God's people, 27
response to Martha and Mary, 93
response to pressure, 10–12
rest of, 38, 43
retreats of, 18–21
return to, 12–14
righteousness of, 120
sacrifice of, 210
and the Samaritan woman, 73
as shepherd, 194–95
teaching how to pray, 83
walking on water, 27
in the wilderness with Satan, 26

Lewis, C. S., 132
living bravely, 104–6
Lord's Prayer, 174
Lord's Supper, the, 83
Luther, Martin, 120, 155

Martha, 93, 94
Mary (sister of Lazarus), 93
Micah, 61
Moses, 145

Nebuchadnezzar, 205

obedience, 12

Packer, J. I., 151
Paul, 4, 61–62, 70–71, 100, 137–38,
    140, 178–79, 186, 209–10
  on doing good, 95
  God's reassurance to, 141
  on Jesus, 58–60
  on prayer, 171, 183–84; of all sorts,
    187; with perseverance, 187; on
    all occasions, 187; for all the
    saints, 187–88
  on spiritual weapons, 125
Peter, 27, 162–63
  on prayer, 173

Pharisees, 37
Philemon, 209
Pilgrim's Progress, The (Bunyan), 170
play, 84–86
power, promises of, 126–27
prayer, 167–68, 204
  in Paul's spiritual armor, 171
  five-fold, 188–89
  four-square, 186
  love-fueled, 177–78
  multiple dimensions of, 170–71
  "in the Spirit," 183–84
  relying on God through, 170
  Spirit-disciplined, 184–85
  strategic, 178–79
  vigilant, 185–86
  See also Lord's prayer; Paul, on prayer
pride, 157, 169
procreation, 92

resilience
  Christians with, 3–4, 99, 155
  development of, 4, 64, 216
  faith with, 78
restlessness, 47–48
Rome, 109
Ruth, 205

Sabbath, the, 37–38
  as a distinct day, 39–40
  remembering, 38–39
sailors, 79–80
salvation
  in Jesus Christ, 100
  protecting and thinking about our,
    102
Satan, 26, 102, 133–34
  lies of, 140
  at work, 155
serving
  with generosity, 210–11
  with humility, 210
  with sacrifice, 212–13
sin, 78, 135, 162, 202
  X-rated sins, 154

sinkholes, 16–18
skimmers, 153–54
sleep, 44, 217n3
    as God's masterpiece, 44–46
    grace during, 46–47
Solomon, 35, 65
spiritual hunger, 80–81
Spurgeon, Charles, 173
stubbornness, 169
success, 105–6, 115–16, 215

technology, 92
    and self-protection, 24–25
temptation, 109, 179
    unique character of, 109–11
thinking clearly, 102–3
Trinity, the, 78
trouble
    as common to everyone, 7
    from memories, 58
    pressure points, 9–10
    as sinkholes, 17–18
    takes us, 9
trust
    in Christ to fight sin, 71
    in God, 133
    and obedience, 83–84

truth
    the belt of truth, 138–39, 163
    need for, 139–40
    standing in, 138–39
    of God, 103, 132, 133, 134–35

Wooden, John, 105–6
word of God, 123–24, 125, 126, 127,
    128, 146, 154–55, 162, 178, 188
words
    careless and loveless, 161
    encouraging, 163–64
    "gracious," 162
    power of, 161–63
work/labor, 93–96
    becomes hard or boring, 93–94
    and freedom, 94
    honors the Lord, 94
worship
    not as we know it, 195–96
    rules: come to encourage, 197;
        come expectantly, 196–97; come
        to share with others, 198; come
        to take part, 197
    for the weary, 193–95

Yahweh, 205

# Scripture Index

*Genesis*
1 . . . . . . . . . . . . . 44
1:4–5 . . . . . . . . . 92
1:5 . . . . . . . . . . . 44
1:7–10 . . . . . . 92
1:8 . . . . . . . . . . . 44
1:11 . . . . . . . . . . . 92
1:13 . . . . . . . . . . 44
1:14 . . . . . . . . . . 92
1:15 . . . . . . . . . . 44
1:19 . . . . . . . . . . 44
1:21–22 . . . . . . 44
1:23 . . . . . . . . . . 44
1:24 . . . . . . . . . . 92
1:26 . . . . . . . . . . 32
1:28 . . . . . . . . . . 32, 91
1:31 . . . . . . . . . . 44
2:2–3 . . . . . . . . . 36
2:3 . . . . . . . . . . . 37
2:7 . . . . . . . . . . . 86
2:23 . . . . . . . . . . 45
3:1 . . . . . . . . . . . 139
3:15 . . . . . . . . . . 118
6–8 . . . . . . . . . . 20
16:13 . . . . . . . . . 16, 20

*Exodus*
3:7 . . . . . . . . . . . 20
12:38 . . . . . . . . . 205

14:15–22 . . . . . 27
16 . . . . . . . . . . . . 26

*Numbers*
11:5 . . . . . . . . . . 80

*Deuteronomy*
5:12–15 . . . . . . 37
5:24 . . . . . . . . . . 65
32:47 . . . . . . . . . 145

*Joshua*
3:14–17 . . . . . . 27

*Ruth*
2:17–18 . . . . . . 26
3:15 . . . . . . . . . . 26

*1 Samuel*
25:2 . . . . . . . . . . 26
25:18–20 . . . . . 26

*1 Kings*
17:2–16 . . . . . . 26

*2 Chronicles*
7:1 . . . . . . . . . . . 65
7:3 . . . . . . . . . . . 65

*Psalms*
19 . . . . . . . . . . . . 130

23:3 . . . . . . . . . 47
31:5 . . . . . . . . . 47
33:12–15 . . . . . 20
37 . . . . . . . . . . 48
37:4 . . . . . . . . . 48
38:9 . . . . . . . . . 20
51:10 . . . . . . . . 131, 135
62:5–7 . . . . . . . 41
63:2 . . . . . . . . . 194
63:3 . . . . . . . . . 193, 194
73:23–26 . . . . . 52
86:11 . . . . . . . . 135
89:8–9 . . . . . . . 27
103:13–14 . . . 19
107:9 . . . . . . . . 79
107:28–29 . . . 27
119 . . . . . . . . . 130
119:11 . . . . . . . 153, 155, 157
119:32 . . . . . . . 158
119:97 . . . . . . . 131
127 . . . . . . . . . 36
127:2 . . . . . . . . 35, 43
139:3 . . . . . . . . 20
139:13–16 . . . 78
140:7 . . . . . . . . 101, 106

Proverbs
12:18 . . . . . . . . 161
13:12 . . . . . . . . 56
16:24 . . . . . . . . 162
30:5 . . . . . . . . . 112

Isaiah
7:9 . . . . . . . . . . 148
40:11 . . . . . . . . 46
42 . . . . . . . . . . 118
42:13 . . . . . . . . 118
43:2 . . . . . . . . . 27
51:1–2 . . . . . . . 61
53:2 . . . . . . . . . 26
59 . . . . . . . . . . 118
59:15–17 . . . . . 119
59:17 . . . . . . . . 115

Jeremiah
1:12 . . . . . . . . . 20

Ezekiel
1:28 . . . . . . . . . 65

Daniel
4:37 . . . . . . . . . 205

Matthew
1:5–6 . . . . . . . . 205
4:1–7 . . . . . . . . 26
4:1–11 . . . . . . . 172
4:4 . . . . . . . . . . 136
6:4 . . . . . . . . . . 20
6:6 . . . . . . . . . . 20
6:11 . . . . . . . . . 83
6:13 . . . . . . . . . 109
6:18 . . . . . . . . . 20
10:29 . . . . . . . . 20
11:28 . . . . . . . . 35, 38
12:1–14 . . . . . . 37
13–14 . . . . . . . 10
13:22 . . . . . . . . 48
13:53–58 . . . . . 10
14 . . . . . . . . . . 18, 20, 25, 28
14:1–12 . . . . . . 10
14:13 . . . . . . . . 11
14:14 . . . . . . . . 18
14:15 . . . . . . . . 25
14:15–21 . . . . . 25
14:22–33 . . . . . 19
14:23 . . . . . . . . 11, 172
14:25 . . . . . . . . 25
14:25–33 . . . . . 29
14:27 . . . . . . . . 21, 29
14:28 . . . . . . . . 21, 24, 27
14:33 . . . . . . . . 196
25:21 . . . . . . . . 215
26:36–46 . . . . . 186
27:46 . . . . . . . . 172
28:17 . . . . . . . . 196

Mark
1:35 . . . . . . . . . 172
2:27 . . . . . . . . . 37

2:28 . . . . . . . . . . 37
4:19 . . . . . . . . . . 43
4:38 . . . . . . . . . . 93
6:34 . . . . . . . . . . 18
9:35 . . . . . . . . . . 210

*Luke*
10:20 . . . . . . . . . 67
10:38–42 . . . . . 93
10:40 . . . . . . . . . 93
11:1 . . . . . . . . . . . 174
11:2–4 . . . . . . . . 174
23:46 . . . . . . . . 47, 172

*John*
1:14 . . . . . . . . . . 65
4:14 . . . . . . . . . . . 73
6:29 . . . . . . . . . . 93, 96
6:35 . . . . . . . . . . 27
7:38–39 . . . . . . 73
7:46 . . . . . . . . . . 164
10:3–4 . . . . . . . 148
10:11 . . . . . . . . . 47
15:10 . . . . . . . . . 12
17:22 . . . . . . . . . 194
19:30 . . . . . . . . . 119
20:22 . . . . . . . . . 86

*Acts*
2:22 . . . . . . . . . . 172
6:1–4 . . . . . . . . . 205
13:2 . . . . . . . . . . 196
20:24 . . . . . . . . . 179
20:32 . . . . . . . . . 147

*Romans*
1:14–15 . . . . . . 179
3:22 . . . . . . . . . . 120
4:15–5:2 . . . . . 58
4:25 . . . . . . . . . . 59
5:1–2 . . . . . . . . . 60
5:1–5 . . . . . . . . . 75
5:2 . . . . . . . . . . . 64
5:3–4 . . . . . . . . . 71
5:4 . . . . . . . . . . . 73

5:5 . . . . . . . . . . . 71
5:18–19 . . . . . . 118
5:19 . . . . . . . . . . 13
8:32 . . . . . . . . . . 61
8:37 . . . . . . . . . . 127
12:1 . . . . . . . . . . 88
12:2 . . . . . . . . . . 103, 155

*1 Corinthians*
9:16 . . . . . . . . . . 179
10:12 . . . . . . . . . 138
10:31 . . . . . . . . . 195
12:7 . . . . . . . . . . 208
12:12 . . . . . . . . . 201
12:21 . . . . . . . . . 201
12:27 . . . . . . . . . 200
13:1–8 . . . . . . . . 156

*2 Corinthians*
1:24 . . . . . . . . . . 5
3:18 . . . . . . . . . . 194
4:16–18 . . . . . 151
12:9 . . . . . . . . . . 141, 142
12:9–10 . . . . . . 141
12:10 . . . . . . . . . 142

*Galatians*
5:22–23 . . . . . . 72

*Ephesians*
4:15 . . . . . . . . . . 161
5:5 . . . . . . . . . . . 81
5:14 . . . . . . . . . . 52
6 . . . . . . . . . . . . . 109, 115, 119, 125
6:10 . . . . . . . . . . 99
6:10–14 . . . . . . 137
6:10–18 . . . . . . 4
6:14 . . . . . . . . . . 100, 119, 124, 138
6:16 . . . . . . . . . . 108, 113, 124
6:16–17 . . . . . . 100
6:17 . . . . . . . . . . 102, 125
6:18 . . . . . . . . . . 169, 176, 177, 183, 186
6:19 . . . . . . . . . . 178
6:19–20 . . . . . . 179

*Philippians*
1:6 . . . . . . . . . . 216
2:1 . . . . . . . . . . 28
2:9 . . . . . . . . . . 28
2 . . . . . . . . . . . 28
2:6–8 . . . . . . . . 27
2:21 . . . . . . . . . 211
3:8–9 . . . . . . . . 120
3:19 . . . . . . . . . 81
4:2 . . . . . . . . . . 205

*Colossians*
1:22 . . . . . . . . . 118
1:27 . . . . . . . . . 70
3:5 . . . . . . . . . . 81
3:12 . . . . . . . . . 22, 118
3:23 . . . . . . . . . 32, 90
3:23–24 . . . . . . 94, 96
4:2 . . . . . . . . . . 173, 183, 188

*1 Thessalonians*
2:13 . . . . . . . . . 126
5:11 . . . . . . . . . 160
5:17 . . . . . . . . . 173

*1 Timothy*
1:1 . . . . . . . . . . 57, 62
1:20 . . . . . . . . . 205
4:8 . . . . . . . . . . 84
6:12 . . . . . . . . . 111

*2 Timothy*
3:16–17 . . . . . . 140
4:16–17 . . . . . . 174

*Titus*
1:8 . . . . . . . . . . 95
2:3 . . . . . . . . . . 95
2:7 . . . . . . . . . . 95
2:14 . . . . . . . . . 95
3:1 . . . . . . . . . . 95
3:8 . . . . . . . . . . 95
3:14 . . . . . . . . . 95

*Philemon*
6 . . . . . . . . . . . 208, 209
17 . . . . . . . . . . 205

*Hebrews*
1:3 . . . . . . . . . . 65
4:9–10 . . . . . . . 38
4:12–13 . . . . . . 128, 162
4:14–16 . . . . . . 14
5:7 . . . . . . . . . . 14, 172
5:8 . . . . . . . . . . 87
12:2 . . . . . . . . . 9, 113

*James*
4:2 . . . . . . . . . . 173
5:13–16 . . . . . . 173

*1 Peter*
1:24–25 . . . . . . 129
2:2–3 . . . . . . . . 137
2:5 . . . . . . . . . . 203
2:9 . . . . . . . . . . 206
2:21 . . . . . . . . . 128
4:7 . . . . . . . . . . 173
4:11 . . . . . . . . . 162
4:19 . . . . . . . . . 173
5:7 . . . . . . . . . . 47, 173

*1 John*
2:13–14 . . . . . . 109
2:16 . . . . . . . . . 81
4:12 . . . . . . . . . 205
5:16 . . . . . . . . . 173
5:19 . . . . . . . . . 109

*Revelation*
4:10 . . . . . . . . . 196
5:13–14 . . . . . . 196
7:17 . . . . . . . . . 69
19:4 . . . . . . . . . 196